# MIXED PLATE

**W E S L E Y A N   P O E T R Y**

Also by Faye Kicknosway

*All These Voices*
*Who Shall Know Them?*
*She Wears Him Fancy in Her Night Braid*
*Butcher Scraps*
*Asparagus, Asparagus, Ah Sweet Asparagus*
*The Cat Approaches*
*Nothing Wakes Her*
*A Man Is a Hook. Trouble.*
*Poem Tree*
*O. You Can Walk on the Sky? Good.*

*New and Selected Poems*

# MIXED PLATE

## Faye Kicknosway

**WESLEYAN UNIVERSITY PRESS**

Middletown, Connecticut

Published by

Wesleyan University Press, Middletown, CT 06459

© 2003 by Morgan Blair

Printed in the United States of America

5 4 3 2 1

CIP data appear at the back of the book

*for my children, Kevin and Lauren*

# CONTENTS

## Hat Trick

I don't always come to the page all heated up to put something on it. Usually it's two ice fields meeting. It's noodling. Fishing. Then someone in the parking lot under the building yells or someone in a building below mine begins playing the tuba. I look up. A man in shorts on a lanai that must overlook the freeway waters his plants. They are taller than he is and he has to squat backing into them, the watering can held between his knees and chin. *Curmudgeon*, I think. *Miser. Thief.* I type the word "thief" on the page and there's a cough in it and a woman starts talking.

If I'm lucky. Or a woman starts talking and I sit for days above her, wishing she'd kept her mouth shut. Or she's talking but it's not her I need to listen to; she's the fairy tale's bread crumbs. She leads me where I need to go. If I'm listening deep enough. If she hasn't grown into a pretty cage I'm afraid to escape from.

And that happens. Words are thorny with ideas and any number of them can catch me, trap me. Turn it all to lead.

I get out the scissors and the tape. Perhaps the thing's ass-backwards. Perhaps the commas are wrong. Perhaps it needs more air in it, three stanzas not one. Perhaps the only part of it that's alive is one tiny phrase. Put the rest in the bone pile on the desk.

One phrase; is it the middle of something? The beginning? There's a postcard in it; why, I don't know. Maybe its size. But a postcard: a cowboy spread-eagled on a roof, sighting down his revolver at a crowd gathered below him. A movie; whose? My mind fingers the image; why is it this size and not larger? Who's he going to kill? And I have him. Or the beginning of him. And I know why a post-card; there's nothing short about him. He's going to be a long poem and a long time. "Cowboy," one of a family of bad guys I can't leave alone.

When I'm working my attention isn't caught straight ahead into the blinkered page, it's side eyeing whatever's peripheral, whatever's random. The poem "The Crossroads" had as its source as do all the poems from *Who Shall Know Them?* a photograph by Walker Evans. It was of Lloyd Burroughs sitting on a mule more or less as the father sits on his mule in the beginning of the poem. There had already been a poem from the photograph called "The Horse," and I had known as I wrote it there would be a second, longer poem and I'd need a large chunk of time to write it. My thought was it too would be about the father.

And that hung me up. I couldn't let him go. There had been image blips that occurred as I was working and I scribbled them down on scraps of loose paper that were scattered on the desk. They had no weight, were distractions, seemed interesting, probably for something later. One day I looked through them for fuel to light the dead father in the typewriter and one of them, about white shoes spattered with mud, the edge of an oil cloth hitting the heel of a shoe as a child walked, caught me. In my mind's eye I looked up the back of the oil cloth, saw the hand at the end of the outstretched arm, followed it to the grim, silent face and knew it wasn't the father's poem; it was the mother's.

Photographs, paintings, other poets' poems, what the woman three seats in front of me on the bus is saying to the woman beside her, the airplane coming visible from the apartment building to the left of this one, its flight a needle stitching the sky to the lanai's overhang, the Three Stooges, Medea, a comma between two words in a phrase written on a sidewalk, how it changes the words on either side of it, can stop me cold, bring me to the page, sometimes with enough heat, a poem happens; sometimes not. Christopher Columbus, before he became "Short Take 20," was a very minor character—not even second string, in a poem I was so in love with it took me weeks to understand it was dead. It was after reading that Columbus had tucked Toscanelli's map into his atlas before he sailed for what he believed was Japan that I dug him free from the bone pile on my desk, took away his syphilis, important to the dead poem, and gave him Jonah instead.

I have written over 2000 poems for The Alternative Press, part of a multi-original postcard arts work series begun by them in the 1970s. There have been many visual artists — to name three; Brenda Goodman, Aris Koutroulis, Carol Steen — as well as poets and writers, again — to name three; Andrei Codrescu, Kenward Elmslie, Robert Creeley—who have completed at least one series of 500 postcards and sent them off to Ken and Ann Mikolowski to be distributed along with letter-press broadsides, bookmarks, and bumper stickers in The Alternative Press mailings.

What intrigued me about doing it was it was a funny idea, and I didn't know if I could work that small. The first series I made was I think in 1974 and the last in 1999. "The Violence of Potatoes," some of the "Short Take" series, some of "Genesis," in fact, most of the poems here have at least a finger or thigh bone stolen from one of the four postcard series I wrote for The Alternative Press.

The ten pen-and-ink drawings included here rose from the deaths of many erasers. They are my cuties and homage to art history and to Vargas, Petty, the *Playboy* centerfold, Marilyn Monroe. They were part of the 1985 calendar published by Coffee House Press. It took me a while to do them and they were not done in sequence. I had pinned thirteen blank pieces of paper to a wall and when a cutie was finished, I took the blank paper down and put her in its place. It was a sentence taking shape and the holes fascinated me. Where were Miss February, Miss August, Miss April? Why were they absent? What did their absence have to do with time? When all thirteen cuties were lined up where I could see them, I wanted to keep them right where they were. But they had to go off and be a calendar, and, having been that, ten of them have come here. They are anonymous except for the astrology that taints them.

Which came last? The cutie with the bird cage. I remember drawing it in her hand and almost shouting with delight at how illogical it was for her to have it. Then came figuring out what was in the bird cage and I wanted to kill myself. I put Magritte's hat in it, a shoe, the moon, a steak. I thought the cutie would never leave the drawing board. There she'd be, me cobwebbed to the chair, her steady gaze fixed on what I couldn't see.

Why a hanger, I can't remember. Perhaps one bent as I was hanging something on it, or perhaps one hung from a door knob and what hung from it fell to the floor as the door opened. "Its wings don't work anymore," is very like something my daughter might have said.

Hanger as bird; the sense of it. I put it in the bird cage. The cutie wasn't looking at it, she was listening to it sing.

## I Don't Know Her

This woman here, sloppy-shouldered,
squint-eyed, I don't know her.
Nor this room
she's in. Those wooden walls
and floors. All stained-up.
All whopper-jawed
and needing nails and paint.
I don't know her.

The size
of her nose or her mouth
pulled up. The sleeping kid
she holds.
I couldn't name you her

if you asked me. Nor him,
nor the rest of them all lined out
and held so still. Unnatural.
I've seen fish
on a string
down a country boy's back
look more natural
than they look, posed close
together, not scratching, not
with the window opened and the old
one there, looking out.

And his handkerchief's not knotted
tight
on his neck like he usually wears it.

And her, with the safety pin,
the young
one, getting long-boned and moony,
scratching her toes
against the wood, I don't know her,
neither.
Nor do I care to.
That suspicious old lady,
head cocked, sideways looking out
at me, new shoelaces in her shoes,
I wouldn't look out
my window
to look at her, nor listen
to her talking
at the vegetables
in her backyard garden.

None of them is worth the time
and they've all
been dead
longer years than I been born
and living.
And the road out front
don't lead no where near their house, it
sitting in the hollow
down lower than that stand
of trees out back
of the chicken coop.

And that little picture tacked
on the wall back there

where the old man can see it
but the kids have to stand
on the wash tub turned over,
don't mean a thing to me.

And the shirt
over the door, you can see its
collar here, I've never seen it
on anyone
or anyplace other than right
there, it's always been just like that,
partly visible, at the top
of the picture.

But mostly her,
it's mostly her
I don't know. I maybe seen
pictures of rooms
like this, and kids
sleeping or awake—all tilt-faced
and dreamy-eyed
like that one, or wanting to run
by the side
of the house with the dog,
throwing sticks
and giggling, like that little one
there
held in between his father's knees—
I maybe seen

kids like that, running in the street
or in the alley.

Even that old lady, I've seen her
too, or someone like her,
peeking around a curtain, the room
behind her
dark and never opened. And him,

he's everywhere; I see him
any time of the day.
But her,
I've never seen her.
That big hand rolled into a fist,
those feet bent double
under her,
that little edge of slip
showing underneath her checker dress; no,

I've never seen her before
nor do I care to see her now.
Her hair
all knotted
and black, those bug bites

showing on her chest
where her dress is opened.
The dirt on her and how she's all
slopped down
on the edge of the bed looking like
she hasn't any sense at all
behind her face.
I don't know her nor
do I care to.

She leaves that baby whining
on the floor
while she goes off in the field
looking for men.
She leaves it between chairs
so it can't crawl too far.
Everyday
she leaves it. She goes farther
and farther, sometimes

disappears in the weeds,
sometimes stands in the shade
of the trees looking out
at the men and rubbing her hand
on her arm
or scratching at the ticks
on her legs. She squints

under her hand and sometimes follows
the road, wagons coming along,
sometimes cars. She lies herself down
under a tree

and everything stalls
right there.
She's slower and slower
getting back. One day you'll take this

picture out to show me, to have me
story it for you, and there'll be
an empty place at the corner
of the bed. And the baby

will be all knotted up
and asleep on the sheet
with no momma anywhere near it.
She'll be gone,
she'll have disappeared down the road
so far
there'll be no time to call her back
so you can show me this

picture with her in it.
She'll be in the shade
of a tree or in the shade
of some man's arms.
And none of them
will see it, they'll all

be right there, lined up, looking straight
ahead and never sideways to see
if she's made it back in time.
She'll be gone,

and nobody will notice. The bed
will be ditched in from having
her weight on it in that spot
for so long, and the baby
will be asleep.
Nobody will notice.

You'll show me this picture
and I'll say, "Look at how

funny that bed looks, like someone's
been sitting on it."
And there won't be any way for me
to tell you about her;
she'll be gone.

And I could meet her on the street
and she could hello me
until her throat

got dusty, I wouldn't hear her.
You got to know
someone before you can hear them.
Before you can answer back.
And I don't know her.

## The Horse

He'd rent the horse and it sounding like it had asthma
and its legs shivery
and its back dropped so far your feet dragged
on the ground when you sat on it
even if you was the youngest,

he'd rent it,
touching it on its side all the way down to its tail
and back up to its neck,
picking its feet up, squinting into its face,
prying open its mouth: horse,

it was after all
a horse
and all he needed was what it was
harnessed to the plough for a couple of afternoons,
he had a hand cultivator but it was hard,
slow work; that horse,

I always waited for it to die the way it shook
and wheezed,
and he'd hit it with the harness straps
and swear at it and say he could surely do it faster,
and it would pull and rattle at the harness
and he'd have his sleeves rolled up
and be hauling back on the plough,
pulling against the horse, and the ploughshares
would dig
into the dirt

and get stuck, and he'd have the harness wrapped
around him and in his hands as well as the plough

handles, his feet braced and his legs stiff,
his hat pulled deep on his forehead,
cussing his luck for having thought to do it
this way when he had good strong kids
could pull better, the horse too old

and sick to care, and him sweatier, and finally
so mad he wasn't mad at all,
his lips tight and disappeared right off
his face and his arms lumpy with his veins
all knotted out in his skin
and his shoes unlaced and full of dirt,

him more buried and turned over than the earth,
stiff-legged and measuring nothing with his eyes
like he had done when he began,
not looking
at where the sun stood in the sky and how long

it would take to do this much and then
that much and by mid-afternoon,
if he was lucky, maybe this part here
and that would leave over there and back behind that
little U in the trees to do.
Nothing. His eyes

straight ahead and on the horse's backside,
blinking the sweat loose sometimes
10   but mostly letting it settle and roll down
his eyes, not looking anywhere,
turning the horse around,
pulling on the plough, loosening it,

holding onto the animal and turning it all
around
to walk back up again, dipping the ploughshares
and pushing them
so that they were into the ground
and could claw it up
and out and him

as tired by the time she made him quit
as the horse had been when he had started,
giving him water and looking at him suspicious
and cautious of his mood
and what she could do to make it better
so he wouldn't be mad supper was late
when we got home, and him saying

if that horse died
on his land, the man who owned it
had better come and clear it off
and pay him back his money
and money besides for the time lost
looking at his goddamn dead horse,
whatever possessed him to think he needed
to use it, anyway.

He'd say it as he untied the harness straps
from around his back and arms and hands,
looking down at it like he hadn't never seen it
before and didn't know maybe
it belonged on trees
or should be thrown in the water
or used in the house somehow in the winter
near the stove, it so heavy and useless,
he spoke

so flat and low with no heat in his voice,
it all burned out of him by the sun
and the work he'd done and have to do again
tomorrow and probably, by the looks of it,
the next day, too,

and he'd heard there were better ways to live,
better ways, with only looking at the fields
from automobile windows as you drove
along beside them
and pointed out the window
and wondered what that hillbilly was doing,
and he was tired
of being the hillbilly
and tired
of being tied to this useless hide
of dog food all the days of his life,
and to this small patch of land—
worthless was what it was—
and he'd drink

from the dipper and us crowded together
back where he couldn't reach us with the harness straps
if he should try, looking
at him and at her, knowing she'd handle it,
she'd even out his temper before we took the horse
back and headed for home ourselves.

And as we went back
and it darkening
his mood toward the horse
changed
and he wasn't so sour toward it, it did the best
it could, old and lame
and sick as it was. The air

was cooler
and his body and legs weren't so knotted up
nor his arms,
his sleeves rolled down, his hat
pushed back on his head, the day
didn't hurt so much thinking about it
as we walked in the slow dark
toward home.

## Kitchen

The sun makes a sound
in the morning—silver—rattling clear
as pump water.
Dust rises slowly, is brittle
and wheel-like.

She feels fingers come alive out
of the wood of the tables,
the walls; they catch
at her skirt, at the skin
of her legs and arms.

She brushes past them, feels
the dust move
slowly
and perfectly; in time,

if she stood still long enough,
it would cover her.

Dust is in her nose
and eyes.
Flies nest in her hair, her collar;
she feels their little hands.

The clock ticks.
Noise comes into the room
through the window. The sun

makes a high-pitched sound that is like
the sound her nerves make;
she feels it behind her eyes,
and her skin
is alert
and flinches
at the touch of the air
against it.

## Who Is She?

Look at how she sits.
That old man, is he her husband?
He's so scrawny-necked,
so dried up.

I bet she blows her nose
with her fingers, leans
one of her arms around a child,
bent forward a little,
her other hand at her nose;
her snot dries faster than she
can blow.
Maybe sometimes she uses
the hem of her dress

and the snot cakes there,
and her children
grab hold of her
and hug her with their faces
pushed into her dress.

Her face is crooked. It went
crooked in the sheet
or in his arms.
It got squashed up against him
one night, and it never
went back straight
again.

Look at how tired she is; it's as plain
as her hair
or her shoulders. Look at how
she shrugs forward.

Her mother is dead; and another thing,
she might be that old man's wife now,
but she was first
his daughter.

That old husband-man,
the sun has fiddled its way
through the holes in his hat
and has scorched
his brains.

She wishes she was dead
instead of her mother.
She used to follow her
down the bean rows, trying to touch
her dress.

And they'd go into town
together. Her mother would look in
at the dinette window.

Men would look up,
push back from their food,
wiping their lips
with their sleeves.

She's so tired; look at how thin
she is. Only her hair is fat.
It's getting darker
all around; she's smaller than
a midget.
I'll be the size of her,
but I'll be wrinkled up.
She'll catch me by my arm,

and this picture
will be lying
on an ironing board
and where she sat
will be empty; she'll have scraped
herself free and she'll force me
to sit there,
where she was,
and she'll iron me down,
making me flat
so that I fit.

I'll be alive,
and my hands will hurt,
and my head will be ditched down
into my shoulders.

The man who took this picture
thought his mouth had disappeared.
In its place was a hole
that might as well have spiders
or mice living inside it.

He thought that if he spoke
he'd make a noise like bushes

scraping against the side
of the house, or like flies
worrying
at the sunlight
on a porch.

He hadn't meant to bother with anyone.
He had his camera
on a string
around his neck, the husband put his hand
on the porch rail, she

was stooped forward in her chair,
shucking peas, the child
tied to her
in her apron.
She had looked up, pursed
her lips, squinted
her eyes.

He had thought only the sky
saw him, and that only the insects
jumping into the air
around him knew
he was there.

But they had watched him,
their faces already flat
and gray
in the film
he had not yet wound
into his camera.

## The River

I was young then, at the yard's rim,
sway-backed, belly poked forward,
my dress sash loosely tied,
the bow drooped and lopsided.
The bright yellow dust,
scratched loose
from the yard and the road, sifted up
my nose
and fattened out
my hair.

I stood splay-footed, toes
dug down into my shoes, elbows bent,
fingers in sweaty bundles, with my back
to the yard
which had no green to it, was merely
footpaths meandering up
from the drainage ditch
toward the house squatted down
beside its two sickly trees.

I was dizzy with sun, but did not take
myself to my favorite place
beneath the front porch
where I could sit crushed together, my chin
on my knees, spying out
at the yard or listening
to the noises in the house
traveling out from it
through the boards above me.

Across the road was a field, weed-packed,
brittle and high, full of grasshoppers
and flies that leaped
and scratched at my face and knees,
dropping down my collar or into
my shoes when I walked there. The weeds

had little fists of burrs
hung out from them and razor teeth
along their stalks that cut
my arms and legs or bit
into my hair, pulling it.

Beyond the field,
where I did not go,
was a dark, uneven line of trees.
It was hotter there,
and lying down beneath the trees
and covered over
by their branches
was the river.

The air was thick as spit;
the river breathed pieces of its water
up into it. If that air
came into my nose

and slid down my throat
to my lungs, they'd thicken
closed
and when I breathed
my ribs would break
and I'd sink down
to the ground.

The river was a hole
and the water covering it
was a trick. Under
the weeds near its banks
it pretended to be covered over.
There were edges of light
cast off from the waves
in the water that could blind me
even if I kept my eyes closed.

And once I was blind
the river had me
and would steal me
into its mouth
and chew me until I broke
into pieces.

That had happened
to my uncle
and my cousin, and my father
once sat fishing
in a boat
and the river pressed hard
against the boat, breaking it
and pulling it
under.

The sunlight white-knotted
in my hair, I stood
in the bald
and rusted yard.

The road
and the field beyond it
were green
and full of tiny flowers that felt
soft as plush
when I stepped on them.
I was taller than the trees
growing on the banks
of the river. They were like
pumpkin vines
around my legs and I leaned down
above them, pushing their leaves
aside. The river
glittered
like crushed glass
against my calves

as I stood straddle-legged
above it.
It lifted up
and fell back down
beneath me.

How beautiful it was.
How old.

My mother stepped down
from the porch
and entered the sunlight,
walking toward the edge of the yard
where I stood.
Her skirt hem was caught up
at her waist and her stockings
were rolled down to her shoe tops.

Her hair
was wet and as she walked
she bent forward, raising
her hands to it,
shaking it
and twisting it until
it seemed to glide
and boil.

"The sun cooks the earth
and cooks your brains, too,
if you stand in it
and gawk too long
at nothing," she said.

Her hair rippled and shone;
she combed her fingers through it,
parting it,
and I saw
dark, wavy spots between its strands
that were children
playing
up the road.

"The sun can addle you,
can make your brains
as bleached as laundry,"
she said, and she cast her hair

out into the air and it was both
net
and water. I squatted down
on my heels at her feet, letting it
touch me.

"Get away," she said, scraping
her fingers through it,
"Get away," but I hissed
and gabbled
around her feet
and she could not push me,
or shake me free.

## River Hill Café

He was two days late;
his feeling had changed.
He said, "I'm thinking of too many things
right now."
He said, "I've caught you;
you can't flap your arms
and fly away."

They were at supper. Flies were all
around the meat
and he kept his hand out,
waving them away.
"Goddamn flies," he said.
The juke box was on, people
were slopping money
out of their pockets.
"It's different now," he said.
"Different."

She had to look at him, how
he was changing it all around.
They were purple in the light,
"violet" he called it.
She kept looking at her hand to see
the color better.
"I have to ease up," he said.
"I don't want a house with you;
I'm nervous about this.
I don't trust you; I'm away too
long."

She looked at him; he was already
gone. "It makes me depressed,"
he said. They had lain in the shade
so thick no sunshine could come

through it, and there were butterflies
all yellow and white
in the field,
the noise of flies and faraway
voices calling
and singing, and her skirt

was up and her legs
around him, and in her eyes
were the colors of cornflowers
and white daisies, daylilies
and goldenrod, and the ground

where she lay
was cushiony
and fit her back. How cool he is,
telling her, "I'm away
too much."

She had met him so quick; he had picked up
her bundle, grinned at her.
"I'll have tah scrub you with a Brillo
and clean you with a garden
hose," is what he had said to her.

And he made her
stand by his car
until he'd spread rags on the seat
for her to sit on.

Even her feet
had a rag from the trunk
and she had to be

careful she kept them on it.
He wiped his pecker off
with his handkerchief before he zipped his
pants while she stood there
all sticky on her thighs.
"Fuckin a hillbilly broad by the side
of the road, I just might catch
something from being so
stupid."

He'd be lying
on the couch, blinking his eyes
and scratching the hair
on his belly, and she'd be sitting
beside him, wanting to talk.
It was all so different.
"I'm tired; I don't need your noise."
She felt so feeble; her mouth
all flattened out.

And those cockroaches, when
they'd climb on him, he'd yell and beat
his skin where they had been
and he'd shake and be mad
and hit her. Like she had something to do
with them being in the room.
He'd tear the bed apart and move
it farther off

from the wall. There were cans of spray
everywhere and the air
was never fit to breathe, he chased
after them and sprayed them so solid
they were lathery.

She'd kiss him, she didn't know better,
it was all

so different from where she'd come from:
it was wallpaper
on the wall and a wash sink in the corner
and a little kitchen place near it.
He would touch on her so hard
and awkward she'd hurt.
"Do you love me?"
She couldn't answer. It was all she could
do sometimes not

to laugh at how ugly he was.
But the sheets were nice
and when she scrubbed underneath the ice
box
and inside the stove, the roaches
weren't so bad. And he got more peaceful
with her. She was always
uneasy with him. His fat belly
and his ass rolled out around him.

"Yes," she'd answer, first thinking
of the new dress he'd bought her
or the stockings. "I love you."
There was a rug
to stand on, her feet weren't cold
in the morning. She had curlers for her hair.

And nightgowns.
And underpants and brassieres
she couldn't count.
She'd rub her hand on the folds
in his belly skin, lower her head
and kiss the sweaty hair around his
belly button. "Lower," he'd say. "Kiss
me lower."

He never spent the night, didn't
come around much.
She'd cook him dinner.
He'd take his pants off. He'd stand
there or sit down or lie down and she'd
do it. His hands on his hips or his arms
crossed behind his head.

She had a looking glass long enough
she could see from her head
to her shoes.
There were stuffed chairs you'd sit back
in, comfortable.
He'd move his hips
and close his eyes, his lips partly opened.
"I'll give you a ride," he had said to her.
And she'd been sitting
by the side of the road
for so long.

Nobody but farmers
came by in their wagons.
And she wouldn't let them,
not anymore. She closed her skirt
and gathered up
her legs
when they climbed down

from their wagons and walked
toward her.
"What's the matter? You on the rag?"
"Yes," she said.
"Too bad," they said, all hot

and lathery, reaching down
her dress, swatting her
on her bottom.
"Too bad."

## Billboards and Frame Houses

They went to the picture show together.
Her hanging onto him by his hand
and a little back. She felt awkward
in those shoes, and the stockings
made her legs sweat.
She was sweaty all over and had stuck
a handkerchief up her sleeve.
It made him laugh, seeing it.

 "Put it in your pocket book," he said.
"But wonder if I need it quick,"
she answered. "Take it out,
silly," he said right back.
As though it would be that easy. Maybe

for one of those women walking comfortable
in her shoes, cool
and fragrant, with not so much scent
on she smelled like a drawer.
That's what he said to her. "Whew,"
he said. "Somebody close
that drawer."

And it was her, smelling
extra good for him right after
she had washed and scrubbed herself
all over.

"Wash it off," he said.
"Don't smell yourself up
so much that you stink."
She didn't stink; it was called *Lavender Mist*
and it had cost her over a dollar
at the dime store.
"Soap smells better,"

he said. "Maybe we can air
you out; let's walk a little."
But she tilted in her shoes
and her ankles wobbled. She had a ribbon
in her hair
and it curled
and her lips were red
as in the picture show.

"Take that grease off your mouth," he said,
and he stood contrary
in the doorway
until she had washed her face
pale again.

## The Crossroads

He rented the mule,
saving out
a portion of his weekly wages
for that purpose, not

to walk behind it
or touch its harness
or even to take the reins up
into his hands
from where they lay
braided together
above the mule's collar,
he rented it

to sit on it, both his legs
dangled off
the mule's right side, his body
slouched forward,
his hands
rested
on his thighs.

He planned it, where he
and the mule would be,
by studying maps
after supper,
smoothing them flat
with his hands
as he leaned above
the kitchen table,
penciling over the routes

between towns, measuring
how far it was between them
with a small, yellow ruler.

Because I was the youngest,
he'd usually let me watch.
My mother did not like me there,
so close to him, and if she could,
she'd send me off,

to fetch her a cloth
from beneath the sink, or thread
from its spindle
in her sewing box.

"Just mind your nose, Missy,"
she'd say to me.
"Let the child be," my father
would say and look at me
and grin.

I stood beside him, asked him
how to say the name
of a town, had he been there yet,
was it all built up
with houses like where we
lived, or was it mostly
fields.

I'd peek to see where she was
and tap his hand
where it lay against the map
and whisper:
"Can I come with you
when you get it?
Can I ride it, too?"

She always heard
and came at me,
cuffing me away
from the table.

"Why don't you stop
this foolishness?"
she'd say to him.
"I won't be party to it
anymore."

"You will," he'd answer her,
and stand up, tapping the map
with his finger. "Here

is where you'll see me."

He went alone
to get it, usually leaving

before first light
of a Saturday, her half-asleep,
glad to be rid of him,
watching out
the kitchen window
as the car backed down
the driveway.

She'd keep us in
and we'd all but hide from her
she'd be so sour.

He'd call her
on the telephone
to say how far

he'd gone and which bus
to take.

We'd be scrubbed up,
standing near the wash sink
by the back door,
kicking at the screen
or riling up the dog
by whistling to him
and slapping our thighs
like we would play with him.

We'd eat, then help her
make up a basket so we'd have
something
for later.

It was a day
out, and the first few times
it happened I hardly breathed
or sat. My older sister,

from the start, did not
like it and although she shared
what my mother felt,
she could not say it out
to her or come too close
to her with her own
grim face.

"What's into you, Missy?"
Mother'd ask her
staring hard enough at her face
to char it
and have it fall to ashes
down her collar.

"You wash those dishes
and keep a hand
on that temper
before I put mine
on it," she'd say,

and my sister would turn mute,
facing the sink
to do as she was told.

I itched
to go outside,
feeling that it was somehow
unnatural to be so tidy
on a Saturday. If any of my friends

came calling, they'd look at me
like I must be going
to a funeral
and she'd tell them
to go off,
I couldn't play.

My hair was washed
and even my shoes were cleaned;
I'd had to stand
at the edge of the back porch
with a stick

scraping the mud
from their soles and heels.

She'd mind the clock
and when it was time
to go, we'd each

have to come before her
so that she could be sure
we were fit
to go out.

We'd take turns
carrying the basket
down the road
to the bus station.
The child
who was obliged

to carry it, had to hold
it up tight
to the chest.

The bus station was part
of a store. There was a bench
along its outside wall
and she'd have us sit
along it while she went inside
to get the tickets.

They knew us after awhile;
at first, I'm certain
they puzzled over us,
wondering why

a man would let his wife
and children go off
without him
on a bus of a Saturday.

She would not
allow us to go into
the store. She feared
we might blunder up
against the counters
or what was stacked
in the aisle,

knocking things down,
or we might be so taken
with what we saw,
we'd whine
and fret at her
to buy it.

If it was raining,
we'd come from home
clustered up against her,
sheltered under a large,
flowered oil cloth.

It hung down
behind us, bumping
against the backs

of our legs and shoes
as we walked,
splashing mud up
onto our white
stockings.

40   She'd leave us
under the oil cloth
while she went in
to buy the tickets.

I'd hear: "But, Missus,
you're surely welcome
to step inside," or, "Missus,

mightn't it be better
for the children
if they was to wait
inside?"

The screen door would open,
close, the oil cloth lift
as she took its edge back
into her hands.

Even in good weather
the waiting was awkward
and long, and I sat

on the bench, fidgety,
distracted
until the bus came.

My sister shared a seat
with me, and she squeezed
herself up
against the arm rest,
complaining that I
should be made
to sit still.

I was always
the first
to see him.

He'd be at the edge
of a field
near the crossroads.
The bus would stop.

If the mule
had acted up,
he would not
have known what
to do. I think the farmer
he rented it from
gave it a remedy
to make it stand still
while he sat
on it.

My sister
would look at him,
then drop her chin down
onto her chest
and fix her gaze
on the metal leg
of the seat
ahead of us.

My mother would look,
keeping her head turned
to the window
even after
the bus had started up again
and all

there was to see
was open fields.

When the bus reached
the next town, we'd get off
and set the basket down
on the bench

that stood along
the outside wall
of the bus station.
She'd tuck a napkin up
under our chins
and we'd eat.

"Someday that mule
will act up
and try to throw him
or turn
its head
and try to bite him,"
she'd say, "but I

won't be there
to see it, to have
some stranger poke me
in my ribs
and point at him
and say, 'Look at that jackass

of a farmer,
falling off
his mule.'"

What town it was
where she left us, I don't
remember, but she hadn't
scolded us
about our manners,

or polished at us
with her handkerchief
and comb, or kept us
close to her
as we walked.

There was a dimestore;
she said
we could go in.

By the time
we missed her,
she was gone
and there was nothing
that could be done.

## Look at Her:


if you grab her, her skin'll be rough
on your fingers. She's the afternoon
moon, big and shadowy, she's the plough
or the tractor
or the chain fence, and she gets sticky
when you squeeze her.
She's the little silver zipper in his pants,
but she doesn't mind

and touches the freckles on her shoulder.
She doesn't mind
the size she is
nor that her eyes get red and her hands wet
when she touches them.
She sits at the edge of her bed, crosses
her arms above her sleeping child,
leans forward, her shoulders raised.
She squints.

Her fingers are onions
and other roots pulled from the ground.
She crosses her feet, thinks of him
asleep beside her.
She has thick hair and dark eyes.
She wishes he was less wrinkled and evil
smelling. In the night, she turns him young;
he walks toward her, she sits up,
holds her arms out.
His wiry fingers pinch her. She sits quieter

and quieter, undresses the hooks
in the closet. She does not dream,
nor does the wood around her,
nor do I,

asleep or awake. I hear doors open
and sweaty fingers
slide into apron pockets.
Her smell is urine, dried and crusted,
the inside hair
of her legs.
He drags himself closer, yawns and stretches.
I wander the bent floor minding the next meal
and the garden picked raw
by strangers.

And them, her family, opposite,
in a row, never moving, like a fruit-seller's
vegetables.
They are less than buttons,
less than little trays
of food handed around to the sick.
They are less than socks, folded up.
She is less than all of them,
less than him
and what he carries
in his morning pocket.

She has wanted to dream him.
And her mother stood
with water and newspapers.
He rubs his feet in the dirt,
back and forth, before he enters.
She lights the fire,
cuts things up, remembers dreams
of swimming, of fish

nibbling the hair on her legs.
They are to have their picture taken.
They are to sit together in a line.
Or stand, if the man directs.
The floor is at an angle, and they might
fall off.
He clears his throat, turning and plumping her
in his mind.
She is violet and silken; her smile distracts
him.

It is empty where he takes them, where he stands
them up. She picks her teeth with a thread
from her dress; he feels undone:
they giggle and punch one another in the arms
when he's done and ask
to see it.

My thoughts are beyond the river.
I look at where it's cool
and well-lighted. Where it's quiet.
The building squats behind me.

I sleep in the daylight, wake, dream
I'm drifting on the river,
one hand in the cold, green water.
I glance toward shore and see
them
brought out from their house,
made to stand.
I hear the oars move in the water.
There is a movement of cloth
at my shoulder.

## I Was Dragged Down

from my room at the top of the house one year when the wind threatened. Momma had heard about it first on the radio and had turned it off, and all the lights off, and would have torn the telephone from the wall, thinking the wind and electricity would be attracted to us down the wires, but Father would not let her. I was dragged down and in my father's arms and I was small enough not to understand the noise I heard nor the smell of fear, my mother's voice sounding harsh and angry as she coaxed at my sister to be calm—at me, although I was rolled up like a little cat against my father's sweaty shirt.

Things broke free from the house, clattering against it. I slept tucked into my father's arms, his chest noisy against my ear. I woke up sometimes and saw my sister sitting in a chair near Mother, the both of them stiff as my sister's dolls. Their hands were held in fists between them, and their eyes were open so wide I saw the whites clearly even in the dark.

The room we were in smelled wet and I could not remember it, it was so changed by the light. The chairs rose and fell, they were thicker than I remembered them and they burst and opened and seemed to bend from stalks that began under the floor of the house. The tables glowed, their polished faces bright as the edges of flowers.

"O Momma, we'll be killed," my sister cried, and as I looked at her, the light seemed to break her face into pieces.

48    I took that image of her into my sleep, and cradled in my father's arms I dreamed she walked out into the rushes and weeds near the river, and was taken slowly by the black water, first to the knees, her arms held out stiffly in the air, then to her waist, her white dress

floating around her like it was growing up from the water and she had entered it, the meaty, large petals of a flower. It was like a bell or a globe; she hung at its center, and I watched the petals lift up and close around her. I cried out for her to come back, but the flower sank into the river. I made a net of my hair and cast it into the water, dragging against its weight. A dark thing, woven of sticks and mud and leaves, rose up and pulled at the net, drawing me into the water. I awoke, believing that it held me. My father tried to comfort me, alarmed at how afraid I was.

# The Violence of Potatoes

1.

She was always mimicking me like she could learn my humor and own it for herself. She was like a monkey, thought she could copy my speech. I told her to quit straining, it was more natural for her to be quiet. She had no brains to show off. The kitchen towel had more intelligence than she had and the brains of a gnat crushed on the windowpane was probably about all the brains she would be able to handle. I told her to keep her skirt tied up around her waist and when I wanted it, she should lean herself forward across the table or the drainboard near the sink and hang on.

2.

She would have told me the names of all the plants but I didn't allow her to. She would have told me rhymes to help me remember them. Some you could eat, some were fit only for flies. You'd have to cut some back very often or they'd live on the life of the plant next to them.

She planted flowers all day or tended them, making certain nothing stepped on them or some weed didn't put its nose too close or its tongue too deep to steal up water.

She had a special hat and clothes and took a plastic pillow with her out into the yard and spread her skirt as neat as she could around her legs. With her trowels and the muscles of her hands she kept those plants alive, each in its own flowerbed, right where she wanted it.

## 3.

"I'm the history around here. If it happened, I made it happen."
"And eighty years ago, is that something you did, too?" "I tampered
with how things were around here when I was a curse on my
grandma's lips." "You do take credit." "Isn't credit, it's fact." "Be-
fore you're even born, that's fact?" "Whenever a hand needed tak-
ing, there was a fuss, the town stalled in its own cigar smoke, what
solved it, set it all going again, was me." "You sit a lot for someone
so full of doing." "It doesn't take but the right moves to get things
done." "Snap some beans, then, help out." "Snapping beans is what
you do." "You don't find them worth your history making?" "I'll eat
them when you're done and get to proper work from the steam they
give me."

## 4.

My nuts hurt. Her twat boiled in her skirt and she put her hand to it.
I tried to shield myself, coming at her from the back. I dropped on
her and stuck. She was so humid I thought I'd have to throw flour up
inside so I could get some friction. She told me I was a dog and
all my history was dog shit. She said I was a burden and had no
heart. If I did, my heart was a boil and she hoped she wouldn't be
too near me when it popped. She started wearing her clothes loose
so I couldn't find her in them. And she kept outside on the front
porch, yelling for the neighbors to keep their eyes on her. The shark
couldn't swim in her lake if the lifeguards kept watch.

## 5.

I had my hands in my pants every minute of the day whether I stood
or sat. "A little housekeeping," I told her. "It's always ready to sweep
any floor." She was disgusted by me but couldn't stop watching.

"Why don't you quit fiddling yourself and pay attention to something else?" "This is duty," I told her, "and duty comes first." "Why must you play with yourself all the time?" "What do you mean 'play'? Didn't I tell you I'm doing my housekeeping?" "You want to do housekeeping, I'll give you a broom. You can sweep the floor." "I've got my hand on a broom right now." She shut up but still sat there, watching me. "Why don't you go fidget yourself somewhere else?" she said.

6.

When I was young, I could fall in love so easy I got bored doing it. It just kept moving for me, never settled for very long on any one particular girl, never seemed to last longer than maybe two minutes. It was as natural as breathing and walking to me. I'd get in love so fast I'd start spinning on the sidewalk. Around I'd go, my hand in my pocket, bridling my cock it didn't rear forward and break my pants open. The girl I was after would disappear around the corner and there coming toward me would be another girl, and another girl. I'd jerk off and embarrass myself in public, ready to fall down on the sidewalk and not give a damn.

7.

She wanted to jump right up into his face and curl her arms and legs around his shoulders. There were so many things she wanted to say to him. She wanted to make sure he heard every word. If she could hold on to him that way, close to him as she could get, she could look him in the eye and make certain he didn't look away. She could watch him listen.

But he didn't come to the doorway. He knew she was sick. He stayed in the living room, reading a newspaper. He sent strangers to look in at her and frighten her with their staring and their silence.

## 8.

I would have turned her out, torn down the curtains of her room, the clothing that was hers from the drawers, I would have thrown it all through the window, everything she touched, everything she walked past, I would have burned it all, the whole house, I would have put gasoline to it and lit it up, I wanted her gone, I wanted no part of her anymore, hadn't she corrupted me? Hadn't she cooled me off and fed me full of doubt and anger?

## 9.

Mr. *Sacrifice* she called him, telling him he was no better than an old paper bag left on the ground under a dripping laundry. Try to pick it up and it would fall apart.

"That's you," she told him, leaning forward and smiling at him. "No use at all. Not even to soak up water. No one with any sense would bother with you. You keep the flies away, that's why I keep you around."

## 10.

He told her, "You want to cripple me, take away my power. I know what you're about. You crisscross the yard, eat my garden, give me dreams. Nothing grows after you look at it. It withers up and shrinks itself to escape you. You come around here to kill what I have. You walk by me and drag your skirt up above your hips and piss on my feet.

"This house is all emptied out because of you. The floor has rotted through so badly bugs fall through it to the ground below. It seems to me even the furniture is scared of you. I could swear it does a little hooch trying to hide from you. I'm the only thing alive that you can't scare."

## II.

Look at the flies; something must be dead. Or maybe it's the heat; they're drunk on it. All morning they've been sucking at the corners of his eyes and his mouth, at the snot up his nose. He keeps the window down and bolted, talks to himself and waits for the dark. When it will cool off.

It's so hot his balls hang down to his knees and stick to his legs. He spends his time lying on the bed, playing with his cock. He pretends someone is watching him, has sneaked into the yard and stands close to the window, peeking into the room at the edge of the shade, mouth open, tongue on the glass, ready to jump in and get him all sticky with saliva. He stands up, pulls his shorts down around his knees, bends toward the shade pull. "Get it while it's hot," he says and jerks off on the window. The flies go crazy; they want to die in his cum.

He pushes his shorts to the floor, leans on the windowsill. No one jumps through the window to rape his ass off. "Only you love me," he tells the flies.

## 12.

He was old and somehow had gotten mended to his chair. All fallen over; he wonders if the inside of his body has flies in it, and stickers and burrs, maybe pools of scummy water all thickened over. He can feel things twitch and break; whatever wetness there had been to his heart and lungs has long ago dried up. He can thump himself on his belly all he wants to and not feel a liver or intestines; no residual gas swells up under his fingers. His insides have all gone to rope.

## 13.

He has the business end of himself, what stays slack, on his mind. Puts his lips thin by sucking their fleshy parts under. And his eyes, he has them stuck almost closed, they'll start to water, or the skin underneath them to quiver, and his cheeks, how long can he keep the blood from his cheeks?

He sits in the chair by the window, looking out. He has something in his lap, in his hand, bound in his fingers, cramped and sticky, gone a little purple with the blood in a heap. What is it he's caught there, all throttled and bent to hell?

Too old. Too too old. And he used to be called "Sonny." That was back when he could bring it on good and often. Sometimes he'd forget where he was and reach down and fiddle it into position, his hand on the shaft, his thumb fanning the head. It was a good young cock he had, sturdy and full of snot, always ready to strut out and give a good accounting of itself.

And now here it was and no sugar could starch it. An old dick, that's what he couldn't take his hand off of, and he might just as well call her up from the dead as it. At least she could strap her teeth in her mouth and bite it off. "Old weenie," she had said, laughing at him. "What happened to all its stuffing? Dribbled away down your leg, didn't it?"

## 14.

What can he do? Crickets lie dead on the path and snails attack the flowers. He takes off all his clothes. His scratchy chin is close to the doorjamb and he wants to sleep where he stands.

## Like Stuttering

well, it's years later
and his socks dry

in the splintered air
and he has eaten your nose

and your ears

and both your legs

and half the hair

on your head, and he looks

pretty good, especially to

the new crop of fair maidens
queuing up at the door

silly of them
you think; can't they see

his hairy wrists, his pointy ears
his long, sharp teeth

too bad

and you climb out of the pot, in time

for the first good meal
you've had in years

there are even flowers

what a trick
you think

and so cheap, too

## Couple

Ah, his love snippets, left for her
and her mop to find. Stamen, petal;
he's condensed them. She empties
the wastebasket of its milky sons.
Enthroned no longer, she thinks.

Cock bridles hand but angels do not
bloom in kleenex. ("Nor in you.")—
a captured voice, reminiscing. She

answers, "These flower packets began
before me"—"And supersede you, too,"—
her weeping washed from the sheets,
no architected son or daughter. Filthy

man, whittling at his stick, and shavings
on the floor, or flushed, or here.
No child. Just these untidy prunings.
("Chips off the old block.") She'd

like to pull his tongue out, and with it,
spine and dick, it all attached. ("You
bet; same flavor. Ramrod stiff, and gold.")
Untucked shirt, dropped drawers ("Shorts;
if I wore them, shorts."); drawers; perhaps

hers, unbroken, her great wobbling bum not
adored, not thrown down as raft upon
the bed's wide sea. Rocking boy; martinet;
the disease of testicles first given in
a car's back seat on prom night, the child

from it, boredom. ("I told you lock
that brat back up in your eyelids.")
"Miss titty-god you called me"—"Miss
cheated-heat"—"Angel"—"There, you're in

my gun sights; what's two and two, Missus
broom?"—absence, locked doors,

the exaggerated languor of her neck
rising from its collar—"Missus Lysol,
Missus Catholic prayers in her rubber
gloves, risen to scrub my breath out"—
"Do you name them as they fall? Your

ghost sons?" ("Wrong bullet.") He fed her
women—"Your chilly air; I gave it back;
make no mistake"—their legs, how they
held him, where they left their scent,
intruding from him into every room.
He concedes. "Okay, once, like in
a fairy tale, a sailor, come from the
sea to a mountain, gets fooled by a
dragon, swallowed, but cuts his way out"—
the blood-flower mulching behind her
skirt's wide face—"And he chased rabbits

and deer? Was he adept
at riddles? uncaging them
to practice 'swimming'?"—"I said sailor,
didn't I? There's one born for every pot."
"This the pot?" she kicks the wastebasket.
"These the onions? This the only simmering
your sailor can do?" ("Where you're

*concerned; dead as anything I sculpt."*)—
and bricks fell, for making walls, every step
she took, the kiln between her legs—*"And
mortuary shrine; poor wounded Jesus, he's
there, pinned to his nail."* Not her

fairy tale: the princess, having supped on
eyeballs and tongues that mirrored or spoke
her beauty, sheds her skin—intact, asleep,
entombed. She leaves the hut to harvest
mothballs. "These," she says. "Your sailor's
droppings," and thinks of what he's quit:

'purse'—its three horns: coin; gesture of
the lips; her sex, at first offended: "I won't
touch them, these letters you've left all over
the house." "Suit yourself." "Pervert."
"I'm armed against you." "'Handed' would be a
better word." And thinks, not sabotage or murder,

or beard, these papery eyes—*"I've angels in
my soup, throttled, yes, and with pleasure,
too, not like Jesus stuck up your snatch,
in pin curls, afraid of a black eye, which
is what he'd get the door swung open."*

The ninth month moon, every eyelash, hair
he's labored at, is in the sack she ties closed.

## The Day's Extortion

Sit *still*, you stupid little shit.
I dropped the paddle, so fuckun what?
Gonna tell your momma? She gonna put

me in jail? This thing tips over
you don't sit still, you'll drown,
capisch? Who fuckun tell your momma

who dropped the paddle you the bottom
this fuckun lake? You wanna drown?
Then shut the fuck up. Put *me* in

jail—god*damn* the bitch. "One hair,"
she says, like she's the Supreme-fuckun-
Court, "one hair, his pants're crooked,

you scare him the way you did last
time, I'm callun my lawyer." Her
fuckun *law*yer. "Look, bitch, I

touched his fuckun hair. Call your
lawyer. Call the F-fuckun-BI."
What're you cryun about. You ain't

bleedin. I hardly touched you, for
Chrissake. Hey, you the binoculars,
what the fuck you lookun at? You

never seen a father, his kid the
fuckun lake before? You gonna call
the cops, put me in jail? Bitch'd

*sue* you. Get your boat, your house,
your fuckun nuts she didn't hemorrhage
first. Nobody puts *my* ass in jail but

*her;* it's the law. You don't shut up,
I'm throwun you the fuckun lake.
Capisch? That asshole's propeller tear

you to pieces. You want that? "Bitch's
fault, judge. I had custody, he'd be
alive today. Kid needs his old man.

Throw *her* ass in jail. I tried to save
him. Got this green seaweed shit wrapped
around me, nearly drown. Fucking President

gave me a medal." What the fuck
you cryun about? A cockroach
cry better'n that. *Loud*er; your

*mom*ma, her fuckun *law*yer can't
*hear* you. We get off this lake,
you say *one* word, I'm the spider

up your nose. You understand? I
get served any papers, you better
get your sissy-ass the witness

protection program. Capisch? I'll
fuckun crawl up the side the house.
Your momma, the F-fuckun-BI can't

save you. I'm a *mo*del father. Fuck
what she says. Child support? You
could set your watch; *al*ways on time.

Oatmeal, shoelaces? *Me;* all of it, me.
Kid'd be *dead* it was up to her. I
should have custody. I do any father

son shit? her lawyer's out choppun
down trees to serve me papers. Fuckun
bitch. "She's a ball breaker, judge.

I get a hard on she grabs a knife.
My dick's wavin in the air, she's
ready to fillet it like it's a goddamn

fish. How she get away with that?
The house, the car, the kid; my dick's
in a wringer, judge. And she's

pepperun my ass with her lawyer, gonna
put me in jail. I don't get it, judge."
Shut *up* about the paddle; it's Lake Erie

by now. I thought we'd be living this
canoe, I'd a brought a tent, a case a
beer. Shit; I was a kid? old lady had a

take the laundry the laundromat, cases a
beer taller'n me the utility room. Had
a come in the front door. Old man'd watch

TV, drink. He was some piece a work,
my old man. You had a large Coke we
got into this thing; there; behind

your feet. Kick it over here. Who
gives a fuck it spills? *Me* we godda
worry about. Sweet *Je*sus; that's one

kidney. Here, fishy, fishy, while
it's hot. Your turn; give um a drink.
You ever piss in the sink? I was your

age, I did. My old man caught me do'un
it. Messed up my aim. Scared the *shit*
oudda me I saw him watchun me. Like

you turn a faucet off?—zip, that quick;
I couldn't a pissed another drop to save
my life. I just stood there, one a the

kitchen chairs, my dick in my hand. He
come toward me? I *knew* I was dead. I
was a kid? I didn't have to do *noth*un

but walk into a room he was in, he'd
have his belt off, be wailun on my ass,
my back, my head, any part a me he could

reach. For *sure* this time I'm pieces
all over the kitchen. But he's *laugh*un.
Pats me on the back, almost knocks me off

the chair. He had these meat hook hands?
Couldn't close um. Work he did messed um
up. He had trouble pickun shit up. You

should a seen him *eat.* He's fumblun at
his fly; then his dick's out. I *never*
to this day seen a dick the size a my old

man's. He takes aim and lets go,
this arc a yellow piss. He has his
left arm across my shoulders. His

piss's splashun everywhere, the
drainboard, the curtains. I thought
he was gonna fill the fuckun sink.

Was the *best* I ever had it with my
old man. He told me never shit in
the sink. It's okay to piss in it,

but *nev*er shit in it. He said, I'm
drinkun a glass a water? some asshole
says there's shit in it? doesn't

matter it's crystal clear, the
asshole's a fuckun liar, I godda dump
the water out because just the i*dea*
there's shit in the water, there's
shit in it. You know what I'm sayun?
Doesn't have to be a turd you can see

it with your eyes. Asshole puts the
i*dea* in your head it's there, you start
tastun shit in the water. He said the

old days? Same thing. Asshole say
that to you? you got these buckets a
water *hang*in from a pole across your

shoulders? you godda dump the water out,
kill the asshole, go *back* to the river,
wherever, could be a *hun*dred *miles* away;

68      you godda cross mountains, deserts—it
takes *months,* get more water, carry it
all the way back, hope another asshole

ain't hidun behind a tree, jump out,
tell you there's shit in the water.
Best damn time I had with my old man.

And I hated his guts every day he was
alive ex*cept* that day. Even he got
cancer? lost his hair? got so he

couldn't sweat? I *hat*ed him. He got
so skinny, I coulda *snapped* him like a
twig. Then he died. *God,* I need a

fuckun beer. The *fuck* I'm do'un
this lake? And in a *fuck*un canoe.
You my kid; answer me. Give it a shot.

## Under the Bread Fruit Tree, the Steamy Head

They, pinkening, umbrellas capped,
had not said she would be alone,
yapped
and bloodied—perhaps a corset do?
wicker with lacings up the back?
Perhaps the arms' weight less
                if tidied into a basket?
                rush? willow?

The old maid clock, waggle
of its continual tongue:
                such noise,
                such rough sighing, and here,

in Paradise,
where she is, her brain pan gone,
queasy in the underwear—will it all sort out?
the bleating? the ash grey quavering?—
                  "Pay up," they said,
                  such bright, red faces,
                  "Your knees,

*spine and sundry other squishy parts;*
*give them; no dallying;*
*no time allotted past what you've contracted*
("Me?"). *Now. After all,"*
                they said, *"here you are."*

And indeed she is. And it
so cool and tropical,
like the postcard said of it—

such fleshy plants, and close-cropped,
a shoulder's width of moving, and sloth
wed to the bed's undulated counterpane,
the opened window's so continuous, so
rhapsodic soft sea blowing:

> "The smiling's paid for,
> tax and surcharge. Gratuities,
> however, are not included,"

they said, reclining among
the banana trees, tiny black flies
gathering: "Pay up."

> She, the giggle-thwart, or is it
> 'gagged,' or is it even 'thwart'—of what?
> in which direction facing? Does it matter?—
> seated, then, and it a chair that farts,

not giggles; there, in clear sight, finally,
where they, or you (a change
in pronoun here, a
sighting in, a
closer look-see) can get

a bead on her, shine her out into the open,
give her ragged eyes a fit
of blinking (needful to keep
the sleepies out,

> and remind her light
> is what it's all about),

or perhaps her golden hair that swains
of old lost their thumbs among,
never mind
their gulped up papery hearts which shredded
as she sat sewing them to her own,

> head bent, hair "Thinned,"
> they pointed out, having been

sifted through
and clipped
and put rapturously in memory's
wallet, that sow's ear
no silk comes from; "*Lank*," they said,
"*where it remains; that bill paid, and others,*"

their toothy gaze
on her flattened bodice, the tits now dugs,
and fallen to either knee
where she keeps them strapped
with leather belts
to hold their wag at minimum.
"The rest, Miss Dorothy;<br>pay up." Such good pals,

their pronged heads surfacing,
a jittle, a jot, a blink, memory
the thread of their eruptions,
technicolor from waist
to floor—or is it door?

Which Dorothy? the one broken on cherry cokes
and the florescent glow
of make-believe's light—you, Lamour?

This is one hell of a landscape,
fenced by water, by starry nights and sun bright
days. Never mind the traffic, the whoop
of voices in the street; there is a habit
here, and feet in it, and no
75

dandy lions grow, so
no Oz. But clarity, as usual
came through the door,
its key iced at the morgue,

victim to you it's said, and they,
arms folded across their fleshy parts,
voices ticking above the ass that's
forgotten how it, free

of its incarceration, had swallowed all
that had been above it.
                    ("Jack," they said, in confirmation,
                    "and no economy of gesture, either.")

There was an oven, and it an island,
aproned as Beaver's mom, same long,
glass teeth, and a doll's
chair beside it, kept quiet
by how the palm leaves rattled
(at least in memory).

Ground zero, ground safely
distanced. And hatted
and booted was no protection.
She's been finked out, caught

between commercials meant to mentholate
Christmas Island out of the air. The fry cooks
at the door understand
crispy; there's one
born every minute.

## Neighbor

A woman climbs the stairs outside my door,
saying hello in a thin, dog-whistle voice
that could split your ear drum.

She must be visiting the dimwit upstairs;
he's opened his door.

What a racket; my ceiling might break.
By the heft of her footsteps, I'd say
she's the size of a shoat
with ten sucklings tucked up
inside her dress. He'll serve her
johnny cake and molasses.

Last week they took his phone out;
then his TV. Didn't bother him.
He's all gristle.

He has about as much personality
as a broody hen that sits on its eggs
until they're leather. And he's
absent-minded, too. If he had a new

shirt, he'd wear it with the cardboard
still stuck under the collar.
Nothing of his has ever found its way

into a drawer except maybe one open-toed
sock and a tied-up bag of lavender
he must have found the once
he took his garbage downstairs
to the trash.

And *he* gets the company. A parade
of it. Tomorrow, he'll come bragging
down to me about what's up there
with him right now, saying what bends

my ceiling and threatens to loosen
the light fixture in it, is as delicate
as bone china and young
as a spring lamb.

## License

From a window in Chicago
a woman looks out
at her front yard

buried in snow, and at her dog
and the mynah bird,
its Hawaiian shirt
and yellow legs and mask,

and understands that a piano,
or a giraffe
would be more common
in the yard's flickering light.
She wonders why

the dog doesn't bark, why
it's so contemplative.

It is Chicago and the streetlight
illuminates what she,
staring, understands
is improbable. It's the shirt,

and looking closer,
the cigar, that worries her enough
to open
the door and call the dog in,
where, she hopes,
he will be safe

from the aberration
that is occurring in the yard.

But it is the bird
that enters, rips
its shirt and mask off, and leaps,
yellow dye

bleeding into the snow,
cigar tight in its beak,
to the woman's halo of blond hair.
It sinks its claws
through her skull
and lifts her out
of her familiar doorway.

The dog, unmoving,
very probably cardboard and the crow's
ruse—for it is a crow,
seems immune
to the woman's cries.

She dies, but not
in Chicago, rather
on Oʻahu in Hawaiʻi
across from a beach
and the ocean
in a ditch
beside a red dirt road.

The crow, exotic
to the island, amid flashbulbs,
television, tourists,
reporters, eats her, wipes

its beak
with the yellow mask, ties it
around its eyes.

"W'at?" it says, puffing
its cigar, "You tink
I one crow? No crows dis
islan. Dem long time
pau maké. You lolo o w'at?
I one mynah bird." It winks,

unbuttons its shirt, and throws
it up
into the air.

## Cowboy

for Bryan Kyser


He squints at the priest
along the barrel of the revolver
raised up before his eye
and thinks of his mother, her piety,
the prayers when he was a boy
in Chicago, kneeling in the cold church,
her breath wetting his cheek.

The camera cuts his legs off.
It is hot. The revolver grip is wet
in his hand; cocked; he smiles. No one
sees it, only his back, how his shoulder
hunches up, perhaps the sweat

in his hair, indeed his shirt.
"Big deal movie star," his mother had said.
"The bad guy who kills people."
There were wives, each fat
with alimony. He had sons, daughters.
Grandchildren. "Where are my
grandchildren?" his mother had said.
"Do I get to hold
my grandchildren? Do they visit
me? Not even a card
at Christmas; I'm a stranger

to them." Memory

should be black and white stills,
he thinks: no voices. The color of the rug
should always be gray, the dog's nose
gray, too. The dog; how many times
had he shot it, aiming down his finger,
one eye closed, the other squinted. "Wrong,"

his sergeant had said. "You need both eyes
open. How many times
I got to tell you that,
little sister: both eyes. God wanted you
to use one, that's all you'd have:
one. And *squeeze* that like the nipple
on a whore's tit; squeeze it, little sister.
Fill your balls or death jump right up
your ass hole, you be

its monthlies, we got to use
Kotex soak you up. That what you want
your momma—little hanky-assed flag
draped over it—to have left of you,
what she puts down the toilet every month?
Both eyes, little sister; and *squeeze*."

The man behind him, his eye
squinted against the image he is
is taking too long. "How many
of these you need?"

"What's he whining about?
Ain't the only one hot out here."
"You're in the frame, dick head."
"The western died with Gary Cooper;
for Chrissake, how come they
don't know it?" He's gotten old

doing this. "Cock your head more
this way, the left." He's never been
the good guy; they should all go to hell.
His girl friend, last night, he had an early
call this morning, decided
he shouldn't sleep, but fight
with her instead so she could tell him,
"You're *out* of my life, understand?
Stay *away* from me." The bad guy.

He remembers his grandfather's disappointment.
"It's steadier work, probably;
look at old Bob Steele. I thought
he'd never pull a gun for murder,
and he did. And Hoot, I couldn't take
his picture, and him ready to hand it
to me, autographed, that time in the pet
store. His face made me sick
to look at it, all tricked out like paint
could hide how down in the world he'd
come. I was glad your grandmother

wasn't there although she wanted to see
a chinchilla and ask Hoot how
he could ranch an animal the size
of a rat. This movie you're in, you kill

many people in it; I mean,
bushwhack them? You a coward
as well as a killer? Your grandmother's
talked it up so much, she's got the whole
town believing you're the star.
She going to be embarrassed?"

His grandmother had asked for
and he had given her clothing, weapons,
facial appliances, hair extensions,
teeth, fingers, whatever
he could garner from his films.
She had kept it all in china cabinets
in every room of her house except
the bedroom, and there, too, after
his grandfather had died.

His grandfather had been horrified—
"You're giving her this? Why?"—
and at first wouldn't let any of it
into the house. But everyone who heard
about it wanted to see it, and
his grandmother ferried so many people
to where what she called "her trophies"
were stored, he had finally

given up and let it all be put into
the basement. But his grandmother's
knees gave out and everything
came upstairs. "You should charge
admission," his grandfather had said.
"'This's how my grandson died in';
'This's how he got it in';
'These're the fingers got chopped off in.'
I feel like the number two *ghoul*
around here. I don't *care* it's acting;
he's our grandson. Every time he's died,
it's here. When I die, cremate me
and dump my ashes so far out at sea, none
of the fish that eats them winds up
on a plate." "Where're my parents' graves?"

his mother had said. "Where? Is there
a headstone? No, there's a longitude,
a latitude. I want to visit my parents'
graves, I have to rent a boat.
Thank you, Mr. Big shot movie star.
I have no grandchildren, I have no
parents. Thank you." "I told ma

she should lighten up," his brother
had said. "My fish got nothun
to do with grandpa, grandma. I saw it
a movie—Julie Christie give some guy
a fish tank the size uv a wall.
It's no fuckun big deal.
I don't eat um; just watch um swim
aroun. First time my life I piss ma
off. Called me a cannibal I watch um."

His brother had tapped cigar ash
onto the carpet. "'They sleep
with the fishes.' Remember that,
The Godfather, Mr. Hollywood wise guy?"
He had aimed his cigar at him.
"You wanna know why I got rid

a my fish? You. Ma blamed you
my fuckun fish. You believe that?
Like you held one a your toy guns
my head, made me—I'm clear here?—made
me keep my own goddamn fish.

Christ," his brother had said,
"I wish *you* was the brother everyone
thinks's the asshole, got balls the size
uv a gnat's, his tube a denture cream
on a counter, the cashier touch it,
he come in his pants he knew how.

*Made* me. You believe it? My *own*
goddamn fish. The story my life, so help
me. You know, I was younger, you're out
on a shoot, I'd think somethun'll go wrong:
a horse fall on you; there's a real bullet
the gun; the shit they put on your face
suffocate you; I'd get lucky; you'd be dead;

they'd need another bad guy, and hey, it's
in the family. I'm not sayun I regret
bein your brother. It's had its perks.
A little a what you get always spills my way.
I can't complain. I usta get laid pretty good
my putz went south. I godda nice house—
comes oudda your pocket, that's okay;
a goddamn car tries to kill itself
the garage wall—solenoid, some damn thing;
I got good suits; like you, I'm dyun from
alimony, my body don't get me, my ex-wives

will; what's to complain? The easy life,
right? The fuckun keyhole look at you.
*That's* my life. I killed the president,
be *your* name, *your* fuckun picture the papers.
My own goddamn fish. 'These're *my* fish,'
I tell her. 'He's got *nothun* to do with um.'
'Wasn't for him,' she says, 'you'd have
a decent life.' A decent life, she says, like
be a plumber, an accountant. Even her,

I'm the jerk got skid marks his fuckun
shorts. You know what I do all this time
I got to myself these days? Your movies,
that's what I do; the foreign language ones.
I watch you die in Japanese, in German.
The whole fuckun world hates you.
All us schmucks sit through your piss poor
movies justa see you die." "You believe

that shit?" his sergeant had said. "Two
tours, only time I bled had a tooth
pulled. Come home they's more hardware
the trunk the car parked across the street
from my house I ever *seen*—sleepun or awake—
Viet-muthafuckun-Nam. People killun
each other my wife's rose bushes. '*Enough*

this shit,' I tole my wife. 'We oudda
here. Minnesota, here we come.' It was a,
what you call, conscious choice. Thought
a man have to go through a whole lot of
preparation he wanted to kill you all
that snow. Didn't take into account good

ole Dwayne. 'Course, he hadn't been born
yet. Dwayne; you believe the muthafuckah
shot me had a hincty name like Dwayne?
Thought he'd be Tran or Ngo; he's
muthafuckun *Dwayne*. He the *same age*

my oldest, twenty-five years old, come
bustun into my nice quiet life the P.O.,
gots a hair up his ass, he been fired
his muthafuckun job K-Mart. You believe that?
Dwayne ain't even a *postal* worker.
K-muthafuckun-Mart. You'd think he show

some sense. He need to shoot somebody,
logical choice he shoot somebody works
at K-Mart. They the ones fired him, not us.
But Dwayne don't understand the fine points
of whose ass you shoot an whose ass
you don't shoot. Besides that, Dwayne's lazy.
K-Mart, he have to drive maybe ten minutes
to get there. We closer, just two stop
lights from where he lives. I'm scratchun
my balls, some dumb thing, thinkun I'll wash

the car I get home, Dwayne walks in,
AK-47, two banana clips taped together,
next thing I know I'm a hospital bed
tellun my wife scratch my toes, they drivun
me crazy. Still do. Good ole Dwayne;
I mean that. Muthafuckah took my legs,
I hope they kickun the shit oudda him
right now, but the same time, I thank him.
In fac', pisses me off he so slow comun
through that door. Twenty years I froze
my ass Minnesota. Took Dwayne to show me
you one phone call away." His sergeant

had paused, looked at the glass
in his hand, smiled. "Sometimes a muthafuckun
airplane godda fall through your roof
you understand the simplest thing."

"The fuck he smiling about? Where's
it say the guy smiles, for Chrissake?"
"He ain't smiling, dick head. Shuddup,
hand me that, by your foot. Don't step
on it; I say step on it? Jesus."

The only time as a grown man he said
his prayers was in a jungle, shitting
his pants in the dark, knowing
he was going to die. Too bad there isn't
a still of it; he'd have it in one
of his scrapbooks with the autopsy reports,
the photographs of crime scenes,
of corpses of the bad guys he plays so
perfectly. It was his grandmother
who had taught him to keep
scrapbooks, who had kept them herself,
of him, and because of him, of real

bad guys. Like this one about to kill
a priest, which he never did, although
he did kill his mother when he was
thirteen by strangling her with her apron
after he had sodomized her, escaping

the police by going west where
he killed homesteaders in their sod houses,
shepherds and cowboys from ambush,
railroad workers, saloon girls, Indians,
Mexicans, and a family of Chinese

in their living quarters behind their laundry.
Nobody worth very much he later said,
his life cleaned up and romanticized
in dime novels, a law man
in a town he had once terrorized,
and father of seven children.

It probably took him an afternoon

to die after the revolver he was showing
his youngest son how to shoot exploded
in his hand. He bled to death not too far
from where he had first fallen, his son
too scared to leave him, fanning his face
with his hat, believing
the horses that had pulled free
from their tethers and run off
would be found and help would come.

Photographs of him in his coffin,
which was stood up against the parlor wall,
were taken with the permission
of his widow, who had, for viewing, kept
his body iced, charging admission
at the door to travelers who came, some

with books or magazines in hand,
to view him. At his burial and after,
two different, stamped and signed
"Official" by his widow, photographs
of him were sold, as well as

fragments of brown-stained cloth said to be
from the clothes he wore the day
he died. Both photographs
are in a scrapbook.  In one, the left hand
covers the right wrist stump; in the other,
the left hand is pulled aside. On a well-lit

glass shelf among other shelves filled
with similar objects in a glass wall separating
the living room from the dining room
of his house are
authenticated cloth fragments
of the shirt cuff as well as the bandanna
the son tied around his father's shattered
wrist. Beside them is the legend the father
comforted and tried to calm his son
the long afternoon while he died.

In the film, he'll be lynched
for killing the priest. To the tree
where he'll be hanged, he'll be beaten
and clubbed, the blood from his face,
arms and back bridging out from him.
Those closest to him will have it in their
eyes and mouths. It will mat hair,
be on hands and sleeves. His brother,

whose ashes he fed over time to his
aquarium of saltwater fish, would have liked
the scene. "You get beat up
pretty good before they kill you," he would
have said. "But there's still
that little problem; you ain't really dead."

"Asshole died from the heat; fuck
he blew his hand off." "Who?" "Him,
the bad guy. Around here
someplace." "Where's it say that?"
"He collects shit like that. I hear

he's got the asshole's fucking *hand*
he can look at it he's eatun dinner.
Know a guy seen it." "You got shit
for brains. He gets *hanged*, dick head.
We're lucky, sometime this week."

Note: Both Bob Steele and Hoot Gibson began in 1920 two-reel, silent westerns, continued into talkies. Steele's films were heavier on action, Gibson's used modern story-lines and comedy. Steele exchanged his white hat for a black one. In *The Big Sleep*, he played Canino, the gangster who fed Harry Jones cyanide, then stood coldly watching him die. Gibson, after he retired, raised chinchillas, traveling the country, visiting pet stores, selling the idea.

In the time period of the film's bad guy, shootists often loaded their own bullets. The bullet that caused the injury that killed the bad guy could have been defective or he could have deliberately overloaded it to impress his son. There would have been more recoil, more impact.

The film's bad guy is a composite of several real life bad guys, most notably Billy the Kid, who said the twenty-one notches on his gun only represented the white men he had killed.

## Justin's Cat

First of all, the voice is always better in the bathroom, and I'm awake, blaming the railroad like prayer: *Give us this day your daily genitals.* The worms eating me crawl down from dear dad's legs to do it, each word a pin of paper tied to it. "Makes me want to shit in my underwear here in the bellies and throats of the cannibals don't even know God's English; need the death penalty; where's the crematoria, the bomb, when you need them most?" Off killing ducks and school children, practicing their bullets: "You'll be a father soon and have the Divine Right to invent new uses for box cars. There's nothing more satisfying than watching something you've killed, die." "Human sewers, sly and lazy, they'll eat their mother's brains right out of her head; there she is, squatting down to take her yearly crap on her youngest, born dog-like into what used to be a pretty decent alley; worth millions; investors coming from their heartburn to bid on it."

Sixteenth Street, walking down from the comic book store, the old guys talking Pound, okay to be a Nazi if you're a genius; after all, it ruined his career; and Céline, grousing in his vegetables; Guerrero; cops with flashlights walking down both sides of the street, looking for a baseball bat, four hispanic youths on their knees, cuffed, facing a garage door: "Random; just beat the guy in the head":

nothing to do with the neo-Nazi snake handlers wake up one morning they're Chinese, Turk, Black, their girlfriends unbutton their twats, take them off the menu.

God is a dimwit, the youngest of four stillborn births before him. It's in the papers everyday for the last thousand years, and before that, you ride the tractor back far enough, catch yourself a louse-eating beggar been shaped to his calling by his mom and dad: "It was good for business twist his legs up like that, chop off that arm; what's he need two for, anyway? Put him on the unemployment is all; this way, he's got a profession": both pickled in the stomachs of what ate them, their everlasting in a meadow, throwing his seed up a sheep's ass; same story, same prayer: *God the pisspot, the hemorrhoid, the cancer for brains:*

There had been a boat, but it caught fire as well as the tree it was tethered to, all burned to kingdom come, all dead and gone, the mullioned windows, the vertical spars, the weeds and grime that had snugged it, had nursed from it, plants, its wood having sunk so deeply into the ground it had sprouted, leaved, flowered, and vines, and creeping things, and birds, and rats that leaped straight up into the air, or tunneled, fitting into holes smaller than themselves because their chest bones closed together into one small cage, so hard to catch, but caught, scalded the hands that tore them, and bit the sticks that beat them, their innards steamy in caps, all savory; it was the Lord's blessing afterall; it was fleas, beetles, the creatures alive in the wood that crackled and spit and put out an eye or two, the wood softened only while burning; good riddance, the boat was a distraction and had only earned everyone near it misery; where was the sea it sailed? and how many, standing in the dirt near it, pissing at it until their bladders flattened, could make it float? It was Noah's boat and good for nothing, the pilgrims who came, beat and robbed those who lived near it, and stole their rags, sleeve by sleeve, and their hair and teeth, and kicked and punished them until their bums bled and their voices gagged, and every hen and pig was given back to them as dung. That it burned at first frightened them, the fire leaping everywhere, and their faces blackened, and the soles of their feet welted so badly they had to crawl because they could not stand or walk, and none of them had enough spit to heal the wounds that covered their bodies; they believed it was judgment, and they were lost forever, and wept, and cried for mercy. Ashes fell; it was night; it was day; good riddance.

Except for the dimwit because the boat is where he had taken his sex, the photographs of clothes and mouths and adolescence he sequenced, lying each separately and slowly against his nipples, then his knees and throat, before lining them out on the boat's curled wooden planking, parts of the photographs thrust up, parts cast down in shadow. Slowly, each photograph taken from the grip of the cheeks of his ass where he hid them although there had been threats of invasion from his aunt and those she called her kinsmen, contentious beggars who traveled with dwarfs they kept roped together and displayed for money, at fairs, at public executions, sometimes at crossroads, bullying the dwarfs into the ditch below the gallow's tree, then mounting it and driving off the crows and other carrion birds, and calling to the travelers and everyone who could hear their voices, to come close and see what death birthed, what size flesh the soul wore when it crawled back to life from the horror of its terrible voyage. Sometimes they draped rag walls down from the gallows tree and pegged them out in the shape of a tented room, and stripped the dwarfs, and mated them, that audience paying more than the first, the males' genitals causing each observer, surreptitiously, to reach down inside his clothes to finger what was skimpy and shrivelled by comparison. No offspring happened and the kinsmen, if they were not robbed and beaten first, sold the dwarfs as pets to the rulers of the various kingdoms they traveled through, listening always for gossip of new births; the village, hamlet, hut; and heighing there:

for it was God's cursed long black fingernails, first killing the shade trees, then breaking through the roof beams to pierce the hearts and crotches of his tiny self-portraits, making visible to all the condition of their souls in the afflicted shape of their offspring. When dwarfs were declared merely secular and found jobs in aircraft factories, crawling through the narrow places in wing structures, the kinsmen discovered the earth was round, there were new worlds, and they hacked and mutilated their way through them until where they stood was poverty, violence; in technicolor; familiar, and harmonious.

The flat earth lies like a flake of skin on the surface of heaven's vast sea, and God, at whim, can lift it up to His eye or nose, or crawl above it on all fours, His face inches from its dirt, moving His head, His shoulder, watching the shadow move, change shape as He moves. He tries to claw it up off the ground, sometimes digging holes around it or into it, imagining the rest of it, its bulk and roundness, is in the dirt and can move through that material as He moves through the air. His aunt, her foot clubbed from spinning, kicks Him. It tires her; she is permanently injured from doing it, her knee bent so that she walks awkwardly, her hips and shoulders severely canted.

Her penis, which he has watched bristle straight up from her groin to her chin, and waver in the air until she puts both hands on it, thrusting it through rag shelters, thatched or timbered or mud-made walls, lifting squealing, fleeing men, women, children up, impaling them, bloodied and torn clothing falling around her, fascinates him, squatted like a bunion, no part of him moving, until she has dislocated the penis, a bronze noose around its head tied to a braided leather thong and held by her hand so that it hangs down her back like a long red sausage. He imagines eating it, his legs and arms growing as long and dangerous as it is, and ever after, anything he chases, he catches, his belly contented and solid as a hill.

His aunt is lycanthropic and, when she isn't menacing doorways as the chalk-white eyelid of bacterial death, she is out in some part of the landscape tearing the throats out of swans and stags and he-goats with her sharp wolf teeth. The penis is as long as a prophet's staff, longer, in fact, than his spine, and he carries it down his pant leg and up under his arm, tight against his side, trembling at the thought of what his aunt will do to him when she catches him. His teeth can't break the flesh of the head or shaft and he walks stiff-legged, looking for a sharp stick to cut it with or a fat stick to flatten and soften it enough he can bite into it.

His shadow lies on the ground ahead of him, lengthening, and by some miracle of cloud and wind he remembers who He is, and in a redundant act, falls to the ground, breaks his chest open, and molds the penis to the bone cage from which it has been wrongly said he pulled the first woman:

"No," he corrects, pillowed in the dirt, his chest swollen straight up like a wall in front of his eyes, "it was not her that day; it was instead a small propane cook stove and a nice fat hen for Adam and at the time seemed appropriate that two things so useful to him should come from him. The woman was made earlier, and was meant to be a friend and companion for the angels. But they bored her and she catharted her ensuing depression into an eating disorder and ate the palm trees near the backyard fence, and standing on her toes, began eating the thatch from the house I'd made for the sooty fat spiders that jump down my arm whenever I scratch my head. It was out of fear she'd eat them too that I shit the clay I molded Adam from. They were both mistakes and I had to change the locks, invent the calendar, and send them both off toward the creation of history."

Which is the photocopied, handwritten pages the homeless man leaves in stacks on the counters of businesses in the Mission. He is an old testament prophet in denim and rags, the first letter monks illuminated into their manuscript pages, working in trance, having first flagellated themselves until they bled into the leather pots hooked by barbs to their skins, catching the blood, later, carefully, emptying it into tiny silver thimbles, each incised with the names of all God's angels. The beeswax has come unsealed and the man with surgical gauze wrapped around each of his hands is Mary's menses wrung from cloth so holy those touching it exploded into fiery pins of light that were immediately sucked from the air into the bellies of insects where they are now and will be forever.

Through the translucent, moth frail skin raised up before his face, the dimwit saw his aunt crouched on the limb of a tree, eating sweet potatoes. He howled and kicked his heels into the dirt under his feet and moved himself around and around in a circle, like a pinwheel, boaring a hole straight up the cannibal ass of the sentient corporate structure. His aunt pushed the branches in front of her aside and knew she would have to tear her nephew into pieces the size of small green frogs to shut him up, and leaped down from the tree through the mosquito netting time is to the roof of a Ford Fairlane in the China Basin. There were saints and holy men everywhere, and some of them had strong white teeth, and some of them masturbated openly while calling on Jesus to kiss them. Their irradiated blood glowed in the veins in their faces.

The aunt's lungs were in threads and she ate candy wrappers, road soot, and copper wire she pulled from the housings at the base of traffic lights. Her body was filled with memory; it guttered and sloshed and had my full attention.

# Verdant

from a book of paintings by Timothy Ojile


He gave his testicles to the creek bed
from which he crawled
the she-horse mother
who wanted to kill him

She dried them against her sleeve
and with a jeweler's squint
looked closely

"These," she said, "are not
good enough to eat
or wear," and snorting

like the epidemic wind
firing past his nose hair
she pried his ass apart
drove a sewing needle
threaded with her stiff white hair
up his spine
and stitched his scrotum
above his tongue's root

He swooned closed
his legs killed
his thighs wiped out
refusing the time of month he had become

She bathed in his blood
like Bathory among her virgins

She was risen
She was primordial

Where was the artist to note down
the scene she was
the lighting so perfect
Look at her hands
perfect too
for bronze or marble, and her brow
the compassion
the lifted arches of her eyebrows
the quivering flare of her nostrils

Yes; sculpture more than painting

The scenery of his mind
was gray and viscous
and his heart skittered

He said, "Da da, ga ga," the fishy
slime on his lips blotted up
with toilet paper which she ate

imagining it had fallen
undigested
from his ass, catching
in the hair
compacted in his underwear

"Your pussy smells
like perfume," she said
"like 18th century dresses
I dream about
when I'm on

the pot." He was lamby-pie
daddy
perky ass
the wide open shoulders
and seductive knees
of beer commercials
the jump cut maniac
braiding photographs
of afterbirth in his armpit hair
He was famine
torture
subversion

He bandaged his nipples
refused her suck
She snapped his spine
fed his blood to the wheat
and barley fields
to the orchards

At harvest moon
the thorn bush between her legs
bloomed
and she thrust her hands
sieved with teeth
into it, and raised them

cupping their bloodied fruit
to her tongue
where he—seated—looked out
upon his world

## Genesis

for R. Zamora Linmark

Created he a finch
without eyes, without
reflection.

Created he thread
and suspect appearance.

Created he chalk board
and egg and paradox.

Created he mirror
and worry.

Created he abstract levels
of appreciation,
and a nomadic tent
in which to ponder them.

Created he a flight
of small girls across
a leafless landscape, a nest

that housed a plate,
and seven cages
in natural movement
toward their captives.

Created he wonder
and china cups teetering
between phrases.

Created he eyebrows
and they enlivened
his face.

Created he sweat, stacked
like firewood
in the corner
of a porch, and shoes

let out of a back door,
tied together by breath
that leaned down
above them.

Created he fire, weeping
from its one good eye.

Created he topiary
and breathless
insinuation.

Created he descend
and make hungry.

Created he vowels
and a woman with a mustache,
fanning herself.

Created he accommodate
and trellis and the silk
cloth on a thief's back.

Created he paint-yourself-
out-of this-one and down-
shifting and see-you-in-
the-funny-papers.

Created he tablecloths
and with a little shake,
babushkas.

Created he dead practices
and the shelves
to store them on,
and headlights—first one
foot, then the other foot.

Created he intention
and ate it as bread.

Created he particle theory
and dropped it as bloat
through the roof
of a maiden aunt's house,

and to her lap, her knitting
fingers, and to her belly,
where her body pooled
above her thighs,

and through them to her legs,
to her flat feet
tipping back and forth, and to

the floor beneath her;
and travelers came;
and their elbows
were weapons.

Created he tunnel
and jump and stammering.

Created he divide
and wipe clean.

Created he ladder
and the breath of
a ladder.

Created he scissors
attempting shipwreck,
and pedestrian traffic
disguised as glass combs.

Created he vigilance
and it paralyzed his tongue,
and every town he was in
turned off its neon,

and there were vans parked
where there should have
been lawn mowers, and

inside every one of them,
women, head to toe polyester,
re-wrote his fingerprints.

He could have suffocated.
Binoculars watched him.
He could have starved.

But continents formed,
and consensus, and lesser crimes.
And they could have been cannibals.

Created he patience—
that thief—and a shoelace
and its equivalent properties.

Created he minute spirals of
hair, and entrails,
and despondency, and nothing
meant to do anyone
any good.

Created he opinion
and stood it on a chair
and draped it in soot.

Created he "His mother's family—";
       "It was very public—";
       "It was all her fault—";
       "So very unfair—";
       "And in front of everyone—";
       "Puberty; who can escape it—";
       "He fed her donuts behind the door."

Created he to pursue, to cast
about, to be alone, to mean
exactly, to be left hanging,
to eye, to abandon.

Created he a beautiful
foreground, and set it
on fire, and a famous female
pianist, and set her on fire,
and continuity, that too.

Created he an ominous mouth,
filled with dog legs
and metric feet.

Created he a garter,
and an airplane
flew through it.

Created he fruitflies
and gnats, and spread
newspaper under a window,

and they lit down on it,
and in their wings,
and on their legs was a yellow

powder, thicker than the pollen
bees carry, and it was wet,
and had black tar elbows,

and he watched it,
and it shaded its eyes,
and watched him.

Created he the pleat at
either corner of the lip,
to lean against,
to look down from.

Created he sorrow—
why? as a substitute
for salt. Then he wrote

the book and the screenplay,
and passion stole all
his clothes because it was
Rita Hayworth, and he was *so*

pretty; what could he do?
He wrote that book too, and
the screenplay, and became
a moving target, especially
when he sat still.

Created he the third day,
and its photograph
was impounded, pilfered,
accidentally hidden

in the bag of an unwary
tourist who died enroute,
and was thrown in the ocean,
and washed up on a beach in L.A.,

and a helicopter landed,
and the fourth level
of the CDC climbed out.

Created he the fourth
day, and it was mostly branches.

The fifth was a crotch
that only knew monologue.

The sixth said, "Blame
cannot be stolen,
but must be earned."

The seventh said, "Truth
has a crooked spine."

The eighth had map-like
appendages escaping
its lips, and he said,
"I am not this"; he said,
"This is not me."

Created he laughter
within his coat
and a darling beneath
his sheet, and they supped

and slept, and she
was his chosen one, and it
was the ninth day,
and he rested.

## Geography

In order to meet with a friend, you must
take a train. The friend has sent you
a series of photographs of a small dark
sweating woman wearing garters on her upper
arms. The photographs are your tickets and

you must give one of them to the conductor
as you board the train. He in return
gives you a small, plastic toy which you
distractedly drop onto the seat next
to you as you attempt to look out of

the train's window. It is meticulously
hung with newspapers that have been
randomly torn and very neatly taped back
together, out of page sequence, with black
duct tape. When you touch the newspapers,

partly because you are bewildered by them
and partly because you want to pull them
far enough away from the window so that
you can see outside, the conductor chides
you and asks that you sit back in your

seat and look straight ahead. As you face
toward the opposite wall, for you are in
an otherwise empty first class compartment,
something falls from the ceiling and strikes
you on the shoulder. With an exclamation

of surprise, you jump up from your seat and
brush at your shoulder with your gloved hand,
having first dropped the remaining photographs
you have been tightly but absently holding
with your left hand in your lap. Again

the conductor chides you, this time coming
toward you and gesturing you back into your
seat. You look from him to the ceiling.
The Plexiglas top of a table which extends
the entire ceiling of your compartment and

is set with six place settings of common
tools, linen napkins, crystal, and what
appear to be, instead of china, crushed cat
food tins is above your head. The table
legs are clear Plexiglas tubes that are

fitted around four holes in the ceiling.
What look like small black dots move,
sometimes quickly, sometimes slowly,
inside them to and from the table top
which you now understand must be hollow.

The conductor stands close to you, glowering
at you with great authority. You point
to the ceiling, your voice tremulous as
you say, "Look, please look." He points
to the floor, to the scatter of photographs

on it, and demands that you pick them all
up at once. "If I could change my seat,"
you say. "That is out of the question,"
he answers. "If I could leave the train,"
you say. "You must retrieve your photographs

or be fined," he answers. "Perhaps an
umbrella; is there an umbrella?" you ask.
"For your own safety, you must retrieve
your photographs at once," he answers. "If
I do, may I use them to purchase another

seat in another compartment? There are so
many empty seats," you say, and touch his
hand. Startled, he turns away from you, and
the quickness of his gesture causes the
photographs to rise in gyres from the floor.

Quickly, leaning forward from the edge of
the seat, you snatch several of them from
the air, rise, and, like a supplicant, offer
them to the conductor's retreating figure.
"Please," you say, and something small and

hard strikes your outstretched hand, knocking
the photographs from it back into the air
where they lazily assemble, not into multiple
images of the same woman, but instead, into
what appears to be the woman herself, larger

and larger, her gartered arms pressing you
backward and down into your seat.

**Figure 1**

Her name is elderly.
She catches dust in the light
under trees and cooks it for hours
in a pot
above a fire. Mosquitoes worry
the air
around her skinny face
bent down almost
to her shoe tops.

She hums and spits
and her husband, shedding his clothes
in a tree where he has pulled
himself up, dies. No bother;

he was made of glass
which is sand and heat
and has no beginning.

Her teeth are sore.
She is no cannibal, nor is she
food for the polar bears, baboons
and wolves which menace parking lots
and doorways.

There was a story she has become,
having sewn it into the silt
at the root of her body:
the river flooding out;
the river drying up.

Her children, the cockroaches,
who infect those they touch
with doubt and sadness, wait,
fenced under an old straw hat

until it is time to drown them,
time to make little fires
of their hair.
How they long for it, listening
to the slow circle the spoon makes
in the pot.

## Short Take 1

A woman's belly stumbles over a small, still cat. A man pushing a rack of closed garbage bags walks past her, glances in the air above her head, thinking how far he's walked today and not one garbage bag lost or stolen or dropped. But there is longer to go. It is noon. The cat is dead and the woman asleep, and he has no one to speak to. But he must not allow himself to be distracted, nor can he stall or stop. The handcuffs locking his hands to the rack's metal rod chafe his wrists, and the leg irons fastened to his ankles break his stride, and the long, curved, brightly colored feather tail attached by pins to the back of his coat weights his shoulders, and spills around his feet, and sometimes gets caught under his heels, and trips him.

## Short Take 2

Sometimes nasty stuff falls out of the sky and gets in your hair and it's usually from pigeons and it's mostly when you're walking in the city where it's hard to stay away from pigeons because they mostly live there instead of in the country because they're like chickens and only eat the bad stuff that falls on the street from what is used like crumbs and dirtier stuff than that and that's part of what falls in your hair when you're walking in the city when you have to go there for some reason like you have to see a doctor or go to a movie or do the washing or something like that and if you don't get it out of your hair real fast like use the water from a drinking fountain in the street or go into a store to the lavatory they got there or even to a gas station or a place where you eat and wash it out of your hair right away what happens is it gets into pieces small enough to fit into where your hair comes out of your head and it fits into those holes and it goes into your head and your mind and then all through your body and your whole body gets fat especially in the middle and you make people touch you there and then brothers get born.

## Short Take 3

A stomach is a sausage and a gold mine.

And arms are always in the service of feelings
which go wandering, dressed in nightshirts.

Sometimes they meet, and it is such good
fortune, they snore peacefully through
the night, careless about morning,

which is a lout and always hungry.

They are caught before they wake up, and whose
good luck is that? Don't be scared. The throat

is such a little door to fall through.

## Short Take 4

Here is a doorstep.

And sunrise.

Here is a scatter of kisses—
such pollen—and the air
to sow them:

cactus, thorn, bramble.

How can she eat her heart
like that?

There is a cage of sorrow—
so appropriate—in each
eye. Do you see them?

And she is chambered there.

And the last sleeper.

The sky is drifted
into transparency

and balances, as does

she, near
what is given to the past.

## Short Take 5

I confess
there's a trompe-l'oeil
in my soup

and a greyhound
quite blue
lying on the bench
beside me.

Do you believe me?

Water tastes like thirst
but goes nowhere.

Mechanical ladders climb
from my hands, having
a narrow spectrum of light
to do it in.

Do I believe me.

A forest approaches
in a sailor's voice
because dust falls
and has a sheet
pulled through it.

Will no one believe me?

The soup suffocates
beneath its false eye

and I lift it
like a water lily
from the bowl.

## Short Take 6

You're my briny feet
and my flat-nickel heart
and my pickled socks
and my slow-drag hands

You're my fisted, saw-blade looking
and my perfect, raw-odor thighs

You make the wheat grow all
across America

and the cows to calve

and the horses not
to be at peace in the meadows

You're my caterwaul days
and my sweet-crawl nights

and I want to blossom
at your hip

Wheel of petals

Merciless

Sew me there

## Short Take 7

Haul the breath up

from the catch it is

a night in the sea

with the sweetie-fish

singing

their laundry songs

## Short Take 8

for Cristina Bacchilega

The man
      asleep
           under the plum tree;

where are his shoes?

In his body's grief
where they turn and wave

and are subordinate to nothing.
      And the landscape of his tongue?

The better to see you with.
      And his unnerving hands?

They practice absence;
a ladder of it.

Why?
      Because he is concealed
there.

## Short Take 9

Let's sing a woman

who revives herself often

who has the boots for it

and the hat for it

and so does; her

let's sing her

in very loud voices

hoping

she's twins

## Short Take 10

Boredom poisons the air

and scars the throat

of those waiting

inside it. Their hair

is disheveled

and they suck at

tiny pieces of life

they find attached

to fencing near freeways.

They breathe

as little as possible

and keep both eyes tightly

closed

believing that death

his bare table

and three-legged chair

is in

their eyelashes.

## Short Take 11

There is something coming

that has to sneak to do it

because it is already here.

Such an embarrassment.

And going

is not its opposite

as the misdirected

so often

falsely assume.

## Short Take 12


This is what you must do—

unravel each answer
until it is question again.

Then brace the door against it.

There is too much grief
in those dry, colorless eyes.

## Short Take 13

It is a terrible thing
to be the breath
of clocks.

## Short Take 14

for Zack

First, there was a clammy heat.
Then, there was a lighthouse.

Some rolled up their sleeves
while others watched.

There was sand and sometimes
a pool of air, climbing.

Little houses had little mouths
and sawdust spilled from them.

A man turned a corner, abandoning
future attempts at parallel behavior.

A tassel of wind scratched the front
of his shirt, and he rebuked it.

And wept, because his footsteps
touched him, because he'd been hiding.

The crimson sky replenished all its
absence. Then took its gloves off.

It was cool, finally, and nobody
jumped. A roof of air spoke softly.

It was shaped like a doll maker's hand.
The moon, and flawless clouds, escaped.

# Short Take 15

for Joan Clarke

A sheep the size of a thumbnail lives
in the vines of a potted plant,
in the voice of a lily and violins

adore it, and sunlight is its major
predator, and its wool is a gray
bumpy mess, and a crippling feeling
of nostalgia impedes its sight, and

it always has a cold, for it is an old
sheep, and came originally from a
hatbox, having escaped death because
radiant in bedclothes, which it has

lost, as well as a broad, three-cornered,
black hat, for it is very stupid, and
night pools each of its eyes, and it

has a saucer of tea, and it powders its
breast and plucks its facial hair, and
has a lisp, but no forehead or mother-in-

law, and is not made of caps, sweaters,
and scarves, or of leg of lamb or
mutton, but of tears which it captures,

first in waxed paper, then in stoppered,
glass jars, and mealie-pie, dithery
girls come out of their hidey-holes,

in each shoe, an ear, listening, and
breath that is not theirs wraps them,
and each is a hallway of trees burning

to the ground, and the sheep shears its
wool, and cards it, and shivering, spins
it, and finger by thumb by palm knits

hands, and toe by instep by heel knits
feet, and birds try to pierce it with
their beaks and fall dead from the air,

and a prince comes, his blue cloak
flying, and the ugly, cannibal moon
is his horse, and the sheep, because

it is a silly sheep, as well as a
timid sheep, wishes it were a wolf or
an ogre, and it blows its nose in a

table napkin, and combs its cheek with
a fork's tines, and was once a bigger
sheep, but a good-for-nothing sheep
that got lost, and will surely die.

## Short Take 16

There is an island, but it is a hat
and a photograph of
a hat, and breath—so tenuous—

overhangs it

as does an inkwell; no;

an octopus
in a black suit
        sewing an umbrella

because it's a comical shape; no;
        because it's a conical shape

and so pious

and so envious
of Aristotle's salamander:
            four elbows

instead of eight—and a heart

that is its eyes' engine
        all drawers of it
        all handstands
        and cartwheels of it

## Short Take 17

for Ann Mikolowski

The highway's been thrown out
of grandma's sewing basket
and is immortal.
Because yarn is, and thread, too,
and the highway's stitched
from them both.

And so daylight passes
and buses pass and are lamed
by the food
gas stations serve.

The bridges, the fences,
the dairy cows all
get thinner.
The scenery beside the highway
crawls into
the little black holes
in the center of every crow's eyes,

because they eat
what's been killed all day.
And there's glue on the backs
of it, so rabbits
and antelopes
and chipmunks
can be alive again.

But night is what owls do,
because of how
their feathers move.

## Short Take 18

If I had a daughter,
you know where I'd keep her?
In the bread box, that's

where. A daughter'd do fine
in the bread box.

A son I'd keep
in the toaster.
He'd have to learn
to hold his temper
living so close
to hot coils all
his growing up life.

And his bread
wouldn't be soft
like a daughter's bread;
it'd be burnt and like charcoal.

He'd have to suck on it
for hours just
to soften it up enough
it wouldn't break his teeth
before he swallowed it.

# Short Take 19

If I didn't cut my toenails, they'd bend toward the floor and be like skate blades under my feet. Then they'd bend the other side of my heels and grow right up my back and curl over my head and go straight down the front of my body like I was in a bird cage. They'd be green and yellow and shiny and I'd push them aside when I wanted to sit down. There'd be pictures of me on boxes of cough drops and cigars. I'd be a wonder of the world. And my toenails'd sound like a bamboo forest when I pushed them together. And maybe I'd tie bells on them. They'd keep growing and I'd need straws for everything I ate. They'd slice right through my toes and the balls of my feet and come out of the backs of my ankles. Then they'd grow through my neck and up my throat and out of my nose. I'd push them with my tongue. Then they'd grow through my eyeballs, but I wouldn't be blind. I'd be dead. Nobody'd know it because my toenails'd keep growing. Not my fingernails because I bite them, and not my hair because I'd be bald, except my nose hair, and the hair from my ears and my eyebrows. But nobody'd see it. Then my toenails'd turn gray and black and get all whiskered like something that's left in the refrigerator too long. And a museum'd buy me. And my parents'd be rich. I'd be on the front page in all the languages. And it'd be illegal even to touch my toenails. There'd be burglar alarms to keep people away. Then my blood'd seep out and get on people's shoes and there'd be riots and they'd know I was dead. And my parents'd be strapped in the electric chair. And my ghost'd watch them sizzle and fry. Then there'd be a parade and I'd go to heaven. God'd ask me to live with him. And I would.

## Short Take 20

Christopher Columbus was a thief.
Then he was a beggar.
Florida was a postcard to him.
That's as close as he got.
Jonah climbed in his window.
It was the size of a spoon.
He had a sailor's face,
all weeds and sticks that wouldn't burn.
He asked Columbus to take it off of him.
But Columbus was made of ashes.
Thistles of light fell
and priests, like fat toys
from coloring books, came to Columbus
to ask him why.
He said it was because their map
had no exit.
But neither did his.
Green flies flooded his heart.
He put it in a biscuit tin
under his bed.
Geometry ate it, spitting in it first.

## Short Take 21

for Linda


Bats, even teeny ones, don't
turn into feathers.
They're rats with wings.
Only cold keeps them quiet.

Wear a bucket on your head
to keep your hair fresh.
And they come out in daylight,
their pointy noses,
straight down your collar.

Sometimes they grow as big
as airplanes. You need a flashlight
and an umbrella. They eat fruit
right out of your hand.

Not the teeny ones, with
the radios in their wings.
They eat bugs, except
if they're Dracula.

# When Speech Comes

I

If you could have played the piano, or danced, or learned to put your face in the water, or stayed thin, or gotten taller, had a tongue full of language to enthrall any audience you wished to enthrall, if you had never listened to your mother's advice, had run away when you had money, gone traveling where you wanted to go, listened to music more up-to-date, been an only child, loved sending postcards, laughing, wiggling, if you had exercised your whims, had thrown more fits, stayed awake longer, owned your own bicycle, helped more with the chores around the house, sang out loud, been filled with longing to know the names of all the plants growing in the yard, you would not be so unhappy now.

II

Wicked, wicked girl, hair unkempt, a rat's nest, a mealie pie, no ribbons in it, no comb come near it; why, why, where is her reason? His nose avows she has not washed, and her dress, all spittled down, frumpy girl—he has no heart to scold her. Half-grinning, she holds on to the table edge with one hand and with the other hand reaches up to scratch his beard.

III

My pretty blossom, my tiny foot, my welcoming pasture, little goat, how contented I am to be near you, to hear you sweat, feel you snore, such a long time separated, no longer so no longer, my arbor, my vine, my most pretty little room, all scrubbed, so neatly cleaned, so perfectly fitted to me, my opening expectant one, my drink so cool on my skin.


IV


You could boil her like an egg. Drag her across the yard as if she were one of her own dolls. You could feed her to the dust behind the chair. Lose her in the clock. Dissolve her as if she were toothpaste in water running down the bathroom drain. She was birthdays swallowed whole by relatives. The old-time shroud, torn open, crows looking out of her. What made noise near her she grabbed in both hands and gave to her father. He was tiny, sat rocking by the front-room window. She uncoiled him, poured the noise from her hands down his scaly back, watching how it soaked into the openings between the raised and pointy plates.

## A Tale of Dolors

From my mother's hands, asleep, her poison chiseled into me, I was taken and kept within a barrier of rain, of brick and the odor of dinner.

Mother: for years I imagined she was inside my body; there were zippers or pins or holes through which she could penetrate.

No; I remained unaccustomed to flesh, to breath at my ear, to the firm but gentle confinement of a motherly arm.

She was a dwarf, the woman who wore the cap and carried the tray. "Hello," she said, always friendly. "How's my little tonsure today?"

How weakly I smiled back, descending the fever the hours of waiting had put me in. Hollow, I felt all scooped out, all walked over and put aside to rot back into the moonlight that menaced the edges of my cover.

"Here we are," she said, putting the tray down and chucking me under the chin with a wiry finger. "My little stick."

I could not speak, not even then, but always tried to answer her. I had invented a system of noises to entertain her, and she laughed and clapped her hands, leaning her head back, tilting her short, deformed legs up into the air. I wanted to ask her about my mother, about that window through which I crawled into this life, this shape.

"You are dreaming yet," she said, tipping the spoon from the bowl to my mouth. "You are asleep, my little pencil."

She was not gentle, and I collapsed backward against the pillow unable to swallow, to cry out for her to stop. I thought I would drown or suffocate; I wiggled my eyebrows, hoping she would understand my distress and give me time to breathe or swallow. The light was stronger through the small window above and to the left of my bed, and she moved more erratically, sometimes missing my mouth altogether and spilling the food past my ear or shoving the spoon aginst my Adam's apple, causing me to wheeze and gasp with pain. It was sunlight spilling in, and the shape of the window, with its bars and peculiar grid, made it the intensity of a gas burner turned high. Parts of her arm blackened where it touched her, and she jerked and slapped, and her fat, ugly face puckered until it was the texture of a wire scouring pad. *O Mother*, I wanted to say: *O darling*.

She carried stones in her pocket and leaped up on the foot of my bed and threw them at me. Her aim, even at that distance, was bad, and the stones went flying and ricocheting around the walls, hitting the ceiling and falling straight down on her head, intensifying her bad humor.

I could not help her, as I cannot now help you, watching me with that piqued look I so admire. She would stay, battered and knocked flat, screaming until the attendants unlocked the door, came in carrying a basket between them, umbrellas attached to their hats keeping their faces safe from the attack of wild stones falling from the walls and ceiling. They had short poles with hooks on the sides, got her under her arms, lifted her up, and dropped her into the basket, slapping the lid closed over her as her body fell inside. They leaned awkwardly, their shoulders almost touching as they turned, went out the door, and bolted it tight.

150  Can you understand my feeling, the slowness with which I crawled to my present age? I would have stayed locked there forever; her noise was my affection; I had no complaint of her ill humor, found it attractive, the flame I needed in my whitewashed, bleary landscape.

I shrank—I think it was the absence of physical contact—and the rubber sheet never changed, the gray mold that grew and crusted my back and sides dipping its spores inside my flesh, liberated and fecund in the mossy interior of my cells.

My skin could not shrink fast enough and hung in bladders at my chin and shoulders, along my arms; it was as though I were in a shirt too large and there was no making it small enough to fit how small I was becoming.

It frightened them; they could no longer show me to visitors as an example of their Intensive Care Program. How I longed for those days, the dignitaries, the ladies, the sound of shoes, the whisper of trouser cuffs against leather, the smell of scent. My face was scrubbed; I was propped against my pillow; the glass on the stand beside me was clean; the tubes and bottles, the trays piled in the corner were scraped and hosed to a gleaming cleanliness that hurt my eyes.

"Look at him, his tears," they said. "How grateful he must feel. Can he talk, can he say anything?"

"No," was the answer. "This is one of our more special cases and makes no sign of gratitude unless there are people looking at him."

Silently they looked at me, their lips pressed thin in their faces, their expressions more and more sullen.

"Was he in the war, or did someone chop him up like that?"

"Neither. It was at birth: his arms and legs had to be removed because they had grown outside the womb and attached to his mother's organs."

"Extraordinary!" they gasped. "Does that happen often?"

"Hardly ever."

"Did she die, his mother? How could she have lived if he had penetrated beyond the uterus?"

"It is a medical mystery."

And they stood, swollen with the image of my mother's organs in my hands and feet, silent, their eyes pinched and moving as though they watched my fingers, my toes squeeze and molest until bloody my mother's delicate liver—

"Was it her liver?"

Intestines—

"Large or small intestines?"

Spleen, pancreas, stomach—

"Her heart. Did he ever reach that far, his little rusty nails, to poke open her heart?"

Yes, that too—

"But did she live?"

And I would lie breathless, intent upon the answer, longing for it. If she were alive, I had a destination; I could clutch the floor with my teeth, pull myself toward that swampy home I so desired.

But there was no answer made, not in the room, or if it were made, it was spoken into the collar, into the coat lapel, or the head was turned so I could not hear. Always I could not hear the answer; always I was left weighted with the possibility that she might be alive.

I shrank and was a nuisance, and the door was sealed and stuccoed over. Flowers and vines bullied their way through the dirt, and I heard them gnaw at the air with their grubby little breaths. You found me, saved me. It was bone meal you hid me in, and how they grinned at you and whispered at you, and the time it took to leave that yard, your skirt flying up and the dust sticky and hot in their mustaches.

You have been good to me; you have pulled me up; you have designed this little place around me so that I no longer chafe, no longer bounce against the wood or swell with water. I don't mind the game you make of me with your birds, how they unravel my bandages, let me slip toward the floor as you clap and grin below; I find your house quite lively, and the noise of seaweed crawling up the sand each night appeals to me, its odor.

I am smaller; I spoil no matter what disinfectant you use; I do not plump up like a raisin when you boil me, the right potting soil and moisture do not increase me; your love, your tender, shadowy feeling, repeating like a salty star, bends my sleep into a cage I tolerate. I wiggle deeper, hear wind, a sound of movement intruding.

The dark—there is a shiny pit at its surface; how final, how almost complete it is.

This is more about him. When he was a young portrait typed by each parent. After lunch when silhouettes are dark and beautiful. She said little. Near a spring road. His hair was yellow and silent. The sound of a lawn mower moved in his memory. He put his hat on the hood, remembered he wanted a boat for Christmas. His mother held it between her thighs. Stood looking. Sweated. Had dark hair. "Get in the car," he said. Her blouse was torn in the back seat. He looked at her from the window. A dog barked. She walked more slowly. He made her wet with his fingers. She pretended strawberries. His teeth ate marks in her. Her dark hair came off in his mouth. It is her imagining him, the distance so painful. His new wife dull and bossy. Him passionate. Always wanting to get laid. He fucked her in his mind, menaced her, his little teeth bristly with alcohol. He wore her, palm small, in his mind, sucked on her, wanting to drink her. Him always a child. Others doing to him and him kept always unaware and not knowing. Bewildered until he was fifty and alcohol had eaten his sex off. Sitting in a bar, elbows up, legs knocked together. Crying his life over and over. The song on the jukebox stale and bleeding. Him in the wrong year and confusing events. TV and memory arcing in one connection. Headlines absorbed as his life. **FIRE KILLS 300.** He remembers smelling the smoke first and no one would listen. His mother told him to be quiet, unzipped his fly, went down on him in the office doorway. She had pieces of flesh in her mouth, pulled them out. His large cock, if aimed at the fire, could have saved them all. But she was too greedy. He could have been a hero; instead, he didn't survive. He told her to let go, put his hands on her head; it was such a pleasure, her mouth the perfect opening. She stirred her finger in his ass, raised him up, her finger and tongue connecting inside him, to her full height, her arms straight out—circus performer, her head back, him lying perpendicular in the air above her, her raising and lowering him with her lip muscles, him moving his legs so gracefully, his arms, his neck arched, he was a flyer, the circus tent applauded, the suction of her lips and spit, no one saw the fire, on line, masturbating, the heat, his smile a rhapsody decaying on his lips, he thought it would be hard forever, her lifting him so gently up and down, not letting him go, her spit thick, down her chin, her throat, her dress wet, saving her, three hundred burning and their death her fault, him killed, his cock chewed so tiny and bleeding, hid in her pocket, she thought to sneak it out, the firemen assuming her pure, letting her pass, thinking her a miracle, enjoying their reflections in her glasses, "Little mother, bless us, pray for us," curtsying and tender smiles, enchanted by their fire hoses, "Little mother, walk close to me, bless me," saliva rising in her mouth, her nipples hardening, passing by them, him dead in her pocket, her hand stroking and fiddling, so quickly erect, no dialogue necessary, moments later, it easily done, him easily sitting, drinking, her good boy, he'd never find her, when he was drunk or asleep he moved better toward her, her skirt up to her waist and held by her elbows, her fingers in her pubic moisture, and him always horny, she pulled her tits from her dress slowly, bent her head forward, her tongue out, lifted one nipple and sucked it, so many obstacles, the sounds outside, curtains and children, women, and her not gentle with him, counting on him to come slow and natural, confusing to him, shapes in the room, and him falling down, her water splashing out on him, him smaller and massaged by her fingers, pushed in between the lips, it hard to breathe, it torture to his shoulders, her pushing him deeper with her fingers, she never sang to him, and she scratched a lot, let him out when he was excited and promised, it almost treason to the woman beside him, and he could turn her around, he could threaten and shrink her, she was his mother approving, he inflicted sore arms and she chuckled, her tongue thirsty for his mouth, darting at his teeth, her biting his lips, winking her eyes at him, mouth puckered out, unbuttoning her dress, him sickened and loosening her flesh, invited to lick, her breasts long and stringy, her nipples the texture of road tar, his cock hard, he'd fuck her dry and tear her, he'd split her open, come quick and outside her, not giving her moisture, he had no choice in women, he was caught drinking near them, they'd never say yes to him, he'd lay her down, he'd piss up inside her, he'd use nails and two-by-fours, he'd use mortar, his piss would rot her, burn her delicate membranes, its acids tunnel inside her, he'd watch and applaud, there'd be no smoke, her hands would be tied in her hair.

## Breath

When a man gets very old, he gets very thin, and if he's not watched closely, each breath leaving him will carry with it, concealed in its pockets or in the lining of its coat, small pieces of his internal organs and, finally, the insides of his veins and arteries. The man will grow pale as moss agate, and his skin will actually look milky the way the stone does, with tiny black outlines like winter trees, which is his breath standing above him. If one cannot catch his breath by the shoulder and shake the small packages of meat it hides in its arms back into the nose of the old man, the old man will become transparent as a lung and wheeze and, with the sound, break apart, his very skin stolen and slipped down the pants leg of his breath as it runs, escaping out the window. There will be no corpse, not even an indentation in the bed where the old man had lain, dying. Not even his sweat will be left.

# Wife

The ants were along the drainboard and in the sink. She looked at them, wondering how they got there. Then she turned the faucet on, filled a glass of water, and carefully poured it on them, beginning with the last one in the column. She wiped them into the sink with a sponge, thinking, "I could do this all day, stand here, drowning ants. I could make a little fire of them if I wanted to, pile them up in the sink. They probably wouldn't leave any ash at all, the toweling would, and I'd have to be careful not to mark the sink. As though it would matter. He wouldn't even notice. He looks at his shoes more than he looks at anything in this house. I could dig a hole beside the drain; he wouldn't notice it. When is he ever by the sink to see? He only comes into the kitchen to sit at the table. From the table he goes to his chair and from his chair either to bed or out for a walk and then to bed. I could start an ant farm in the sink. What I should do, instead of drowning them, is gather them up and seed his chair with them. That might make him look up. He'd at least blink his eyes. I could put ants in his chair every day until he wouldn't go near it anymore. I could put them in his newspaper, too. They'd crawl up his sleeves while he was holding it."

## Woman

There is a woman standing in a doorway. She has sallow skin and hair like metal shavings. Her dress fits her as though it had been dropped onto her from the ceiling. She is fatigued and would like to sit down, but there is only one chair in the room she faces and it is pulled up to a table and a sleeper sits in it bent forward, his arms folded upon the table and his head rested upon his arms. There is a window near the table, and the curtain blows out from it, touching the fingers of the hand nearest it. It is raining. There is no fragrance in the rain, no scent which is clear and distinguishable. The woman in the doorway touches her face, remembering how as a girl she liked to walk in the rain with her head turned up into it, her fleshy tongue escaped and protuberant between her open lips, catching the rain into her mouth.

## The Clothesline

Grandma hung her slimpsy things out
in the yard where the wind
could flirt them,
climb inside
and fill them out.

Do you know
Grandpa used to sit
on the back porch
just to watch
that clothesline?
The wind playing
in her big saggy bloomers?

"It ain't lady-like," he'd say.
"That wind
fiddles those underthings
just as
it pleases."

He'd get the rake
from the side of the house,
and whenever the wind

tumbled
headfirst
into Grandma's underthings,
making them blossom,
he'd swat them.

When he was in the house,
I'd catch him
peeking out
the window. He'd have his hand

at the curtain
like he was straightening it,
but his head

would be poked forward,
his nose to the glass
and his gaze fixed

on the petticoats,
the little frilly chemise,
the stockings waving

from their one pin.

## What He Wanted

People use a man's death to take advantage of him, to come upon him when he cannot protect himself.

They lay him out for viewing, flat on his back, with his eyes closed.

It robs a man of his dignity to be treated like he was some woman's prize silverware: all polished up and shown off before it's put away.

I've never in my life been looked down on by anyone, and blamed if I'll let it happen to me when I'm dead.

I want my coffin stood up on its end with me in it, sitting on one of my own kitchen chairs. And I don't want to be duded up in stiff collars and itchy pants. I want to sit buck-naked on that chair, with my right ankle on my left thigh and my right knee stuck out. The coffin will have to be built to hold me like that because that's what I want.

And I want my eyes left open; it's the only funeral I'll ever have, and I don't want to miss any part of it.

I want the parlor set up with the chairs facing me so that those gathered to pay me their last respects can look at me and I can look at them. The preacher will have to stand off to one side.

And I don't want your mother there; I've never cared for her. When she comes to the door, turn her away.

I will make a list of others I will not have there. You keep them away.

When it's done, I want two holes drilled on either side of the coffin, up near where my eyes are, and I want two long tubes, like the periscopes they have on submarines, fastened to the outside of the coffin right over where those holes are.

I want to be buried near the grapevines in a hole dug straight down like you dig a post hole. And I want those long tubes braced and the dirt packed up tight around them to hold them firm.

They should be about knee-level above the ground. I want one facing toward the house and the other facing toward the road.

They will be my marker.

## Do You Know What They Did to Grandpa?

They put his box
on the river; they put it
on the river, and him in it,

dressed up so dandy,
so peaceful in all that bedding,
with his eyes shut,
and his nose shut;

they sailed him out
on the river,
like he was in a boat;
they nailed it up,
the air
in it fluffing out
his pillow, fattening out
the handerchief in his pocket;
they took it

down from their shoulders,
there in the reeds
by the bank
of the river; they took it down,

and he said nothing,
nor did he stir about inside it,
although he had a fear

of the water, and he never
went near it; they put him
down beside it,
letting go the little brass handles,

and they scooped water up
and onto their heads with their hands
as they kneeled
beside it, and they splashed

it up at one another,
but there was hardly any fun
in it,

Grandpa so still
lying beside them.

And they would have put it
on fire
and seen how long
it would float
before the water took it;

they would have siphoned gasoline
from a car
or looked
for dry rushes and twigs to set upon it
and then light it up;

they talked of it
squatting there beside him,
breaking off sawgrass
from around their feet
and putting it between their teeth;

he wouldn't float long, and the fire
would not consume him;
the water
would fume and fret
at the box, lap up
against it,

and the wood
would soak through; he'd
wash right out
of the box,
and even his corpse would cry out
in fear
of the water taking him
under.

They decided against it;
the nails would not be fast
in the wood
although the wood would swell up
from the water;
the wood would move against itself,
and the nails

would twist free
from the holes,
and the box

collapse
upon the water;
all the fancy bedding
Grandpa had ordered special

for this occasion
would be yanked and torn,
first by the box
coming apart and then
by the currents

fighting it this way
and that.

## The Bed He Dreamed Himself Into

I

Grandpa batted his eyelids
closed
and scratched his fingers
down the sheet
that covered him.
His body shook.
Then it broke.

They put him together
with glue
and snugged him down
into the box.
Whatever stuck out,
they cut off
to make him look tidy.

But they were fooled;

Grandpa had tricked them.
He kept still,
but I heard his rattly breath
and saw
his eyes move
underneath
his eyelids.

## II

What was it
he wanted?

Was he thirsty?

He was the size
of a pin;
he was the size
of a billy goat's chin
whisker.

So pale he looked
and flattened out,
tucked down
in that coffin.

## III

Grandpa used to be
round-bellied.

That was summer,
and there were vegetables
everywhere,
the air

fat
with baseball,
shucked peas, and car
tinkering.

Grandpa
would sleep
in his chair

or stand
by the screen door

or soak
in the bathtub, dreaming


IV

it was the river.

I'd hear him
whispering
to the fish

that spilled down
from his arms

or to the weeds
he saw
in the wallpaper

their long shadows
bending down
to bleed
into the water
around him.

V

He drifted off. Sunlight

touched him, and an odor
of flowers came to him.

He opened his eyes,
sniffing.
Were they roses?
Had they been cut
for him?

## Inheritance

They made Grandpa drunk
his laughter mixed
with other noises

They bound him
carried him to the meat house

where they cut
his feet off
and pierced his legs
with wires

There were ropes
hanging down
from a rafter
and they tied
the wires to his legs
pulled him up

They slit his throat
catching his blood
in a bowl

To steady him
they braced him
with lumber
and split his breastbone
with a small ax
and cut him open

They gutted him
separating his heart
and liver
from the other organs
tamping up the blood
with dry rags
to keep his taste sweet

They flailed
and quartered him
put the meat
to soak in water

They pegged his skin
to the ground
and scraped it clean

They cut the meat
into small pieces
removing the bones

Some of it
was cooked
and stuffed into bags
of cherry
and grape leaves

Other of it
was cut up small
enough to fit
into pint jars

and was pickled
after it had been rubbed
with white vinegar
white pepper
and the oils
of cinnamon
and clove

## November

He could not open his eyes
and would have laughed,
but there was no memory
fit for it.

He was in a closet, a long
thin room, and he could not stir
from it or kick against it.

The sunlight—how wicked
it was, creeping on his cheeks,
sitting on his nose.
He hummed. He listened.

Where was she?
That old long-rumped woman
who was like sugar to him?
Why wasn't she there?
Her hot perfume, her lips.
Why wasn't she all lumped over
before him?

Where was her respect,
her fidgeting, her nose
all stuffed up?

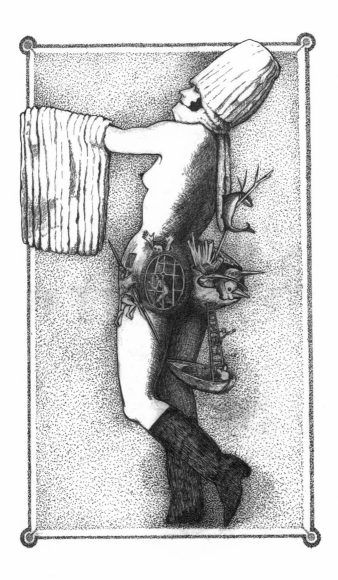

## Winter:

I.

Can there be another I, another wall, snow,
fence, straw, wet
in the line the eye

travels, entering or leaving
morning,
then afternoon,
then hills, later, small hallways

where music forgets its purpose,
its memory? Which tree, swallowing
voices held
between teeth long enough, accompanies
forgetfulness? I have been

I, and later, there was sound.
Hope and refusal were observers,
trembling

by a bridge, yes, wide as a knife,
visible in clouds. I am care-

ful here, continuing; it is difficult
to do this,
talk as accompaniment, as music
that feathers the small hairs
on the ridge of the ear.

There is a sink, how speak it,
near the room's corner, small,
evocative, a shadow
curving near it.
There was I, hand, knuckle, no more,
perhaps, than distant

figures crossing landscape
from photograph to
photograph, a perfect wind
drowsing above them.

I had been I, its
imitation, differently
weighted, descended from a familiar
shoulder

to hands, to her
as she watched, bareheaded,
deceptively near.

2.

the window closed and locked
as usual
his reflection
what her eye does

imprint
the tongue as organ of speech
and taste
what she
the spoon lifted to her lips
desires

there was a photograph she looked at
and all the wanting it cost
clip by clip
falling away

and a pond of flies
or was it figure leaning down
a distortion of heat

what desire is
how it stays locked
a blue transparency across the eye

patterns exhaust
the stealing toward him
her shoes
like clocks across the floor how

the body
before it's touched
the I

abstracted
as the heart lascivious
the heart where the eye

listens
the size of a thimble
and shadow carried
as age moves

backward from her legs
where she turning
sees it move
the way a boat moves
repeated because wood shavings

3.

The heart is sack-like,
is it not? and in each
of its disguises
assumes a forgetfulness
which becomes landscape
the eye rejects. As it should.

Memory, suspended between
two distances, both abandoned,
is like the shadow

of a hand drifting above small
objects on a white table.

She, a thorn above a collar,
an injury coughed
into a handkerchief—
how monotonous, how gray—

lifts her gaze to the shifting
randomness of light, which,

however briefly, conjoins
disparate enclosures. The cup

between her hands, its
elliptic mouth—trivial,
is it not? and the heat
between the surfaces, she absent

to it. There is an unlit arch—
brick, stone—that frames
a doorway, her eye, by blinking,

extinguishes. As it should,
for it is the body's appetite,
and fragile.

4.

there was a photograph
a girl in a snowsuit (made of snow so
suited?)
photograph
the size of an adult hand
then the post (post as in? by the fence
as in? bounded by)
posted someone, there is someone
playing the drums, an apartment below
this one
scattered sound
she was smiling arms, up, someone
(received by post)
behind her, perhaps her father a very

small. figure (figured, the way memory is
then cut by noise
that changes it) she was smiling
was it returned
which book or shelf
perhaps drawer, somewhere here, in

(here, there is no snow sunlight.
crushes you) there was
a photograph and sent

then received and possibly not
returned (who was? behind her
father) farther back
what history becomes the window a.
measurement of time
as well as dislocation
photograph

having fallen away
and then in. memory
which approximates (because lying beside)
absence

5.

And she sat
pickery with sweat
in the float her body was all around her
water her
self water she
sat tongue hair fingers floating in the
afternoon lace
curtains her elbows
teeth shiny and
caught at him catching
her
pudding
dumpling
sweet sweet pie

6.

Desire conjectures beauty.
Swims like a toad at the root.
Of a house.
Goaty smell, a knot.

She lifts her head.

There is a gate above it.
A category of light.
Skin encircling become.

Window.

A wide scarred hat.
Mistaken as key.
Her twin.
A diver come to a closed and barred door.
Lighted, perhaps, like a wick's glass hat.

Where she in her hazard, in her blue fingers and tongue,
where she, perhaps, first mimicked as hand, where she
having listened, having leaned up from her sleep,
having peered between its spined branches—she—tenuous;

a landscape of water.
The long black bell
of a skirt.

~

Kisses tarnish the name the mustache paints on her lips. She, an
    underwater
thing, blemished by closed eyes, entrapped in what is caught-after by
metal-gray eyes watching her evaporate the light he so quickly
    leaves on
her face, a ribbon of breath—his shadow—staining her.

Conceived by his heart.

And so, swallowed.

Her dreams sour milk and mold.
The window's throat scars her, as does
its distance.

She is a landscape of hands, and the morning lies furred and
    glistening,
and she gazes out from it, hidden by her hair branching down.
    Fingers of it.

And he wanted, the radio said: Determined.

What he had stared at.                      As in her.
                                   Eyes tongued over—
                     such muscular heat: to its

                                 elbow—
               where sleep rattled in its tight
             black dress; then fell, immersed in

entangling

the humid, scented.    face.

undressed, every        branch, the pillow shadowed by it

mistaken by it,
how it hinged, and how he cleaved the air
unlocked himself

a whorl of petals ascending her spoon's cold blue lip

Where he had lain.
Where she had tilted him up.
All afternoon on the back stoop.
Breasts pillowed in her lap.

And I want nothing.
And she held him.

~

The ash-heap girl with metal rings at the center of each eye is sewn
to the bright red comb of a rooster married to a fence of water it
pushes with its beak. Where sleep climbs out. As does distance. It is
a postcard trick she has lifted up from the wide hem of her skirt.
Where he fishes his pocket out. Its amber eye. And the moon asleep,
its feathery, damp mouth. What widows have the swine herd, pig-
boy let go from his having fallen through them?

And she,
approaching taller than the rake he leans against, is closure, having
been pushed, since waist high, toward the resonance of grief he
desires her to master. Having rivers of it stitched to the spillage of
each eye. And she swallowed him, where he stepped and teetered;
then blurred. His eel voice had climbed down from where silence
hid and had lodged in the door's pale water.

She is a shovel of air, a thick cord of smoke. She is night dropped
from the roof, tar all over it. Her ears are jars of light. Her eyes. Her

nose. Her bony lips. His shadow curls above her. Where desire scars
her. Angel, dragonfly, hammer; how shall she find him?

~

Captive, she is fallow
as a winter field and was first called
"daughter," said
carefully
to a man, his fingers tented
before his face,
mud-caked boots crossed
above the porch's plank flooring;
"daughter";

who greeted him,
wastebasket that she was,
cemetery,
surprise: "daughter";

who tore like paper,
who stumbled
from his eye, the stitch marks
here
where he flung
his hat, where he
put his feet

until, chalk-white
and porous, crows came,
and butterflies.

Little chatterbox, little
sausage, she sleeps
in his shoe, dreaming

that his hand, when
he lifted it up
into the light's glare, was
a screen of water

down which he
never comes. Little bratty
kid, little sugar
bun, his skull
perfumes the gate post

as does the silence
which chambers him, his fingers

a necklace of leaves fallen
to the arbor path,
the door sill, the kitchen floor—
such pious moths—lifted

every crumb
toward the lamp's perfect light.

~

She has come from the root of the house.
To close and bar it.
Where he is unlocked.
And his lips.
Held up by mops and hairbrushes.
There is a chimney of bread.
Across a threshold.
Which undresses him.
From her skirt where he has spilled.
Where she has been asleep.
And a steady map and a blind peddler.

It is Time that engorges her.
And perhaps a chair.
Her heart is killed from her.
Like accident.
It is draped and grazes.
Like quartered silk, and injury.
And its mysterious walls.
His hinged boots and the wreckage language makes.
All mixed together and funneled down the hall
                                        to climb her back
                              and pull her hair across her face.
                                        Her gaze; how
                                             it hesitates.
                        Scraped loose, turned out by the hedgerow.

Even though sun in muddy sleep, even though the heart bites what
  comes near it.

Such mildewed eyes. Sunlight drifts. There are petals of it across
  the floor.

7.

Toy size; she sees
                    him
again; he is

toy size.  What is
happening, is she.  sees.  him.  again.

and blinks, finding
that she can. And buried
                        to one side of where

he is. is
a dead
and ancient grave. And she

confused by it hides
                        it

in her stocking because
there is a pressure to do this. With her eyes.
And other things.

To do this. And he, is to
one side.  of it.  and
it is buried there

8.

Night is soiled and blue, tricked up
with curtains and steamy eyelashes.
The kitchen wall is like a blank shoulder.
And he a fly renouncing it.
A tweak, a brush of the hand, and spilled
light, like erasure wherever
the gaze descends. And it does—drawn,
watery and pale. There is a slate

roof above a simple house, and a woman,
like a small hill of marble, lying in
a field where a painter forgets
to paint her, captured as he is in his
stalled, lifted hands. The canvas

on the easel behind him is stitched
to the eyes of the man inside the house,
who is like a tiny claw, watching.
And he lies down, captive of his grief,

and becomes a marsh and a blood red
sky, and it is murder, most
odious, and as hostage to it,
the woman rises, and the stalks
of her legs pierce him, and she feeds him

her clothing which lies above him
like braille on a page. The sun floats

like a hat above them, and it is hopeless.
A bandit feeds them ice he has carefully
reconstructed from their silences.
It dissolves on his fingers and he is
a lattice of mirrors from which their
endlessly edited lives will not bloom.

9.

for Margo



It is midday and she an old woman
standing by a highway, watching
a hundred cars step slowly toward
what appears to be distance. She
has an untidy, gray face, and
hair that is wispy, thinned out,
scratched off, and her body climbs

down from her eyes as does the
traffic. She has no fingernails;
they've been scuffed off and are
shavings dribbled down the front
of stiff overalls covering her

body. Cars push free from the
pupils of her eyes—one headlight,
the grill, the other headlight,
the front bumper, the fender, the
windshield. Exhaust fumes sluice
her tongue, coat her lungs. Copies

of her body fence both sides of the
highway, and like it and the cars,
diminish in size, until dots, then
absence. A small, green net empties

her—a girl, like a braid of music,
seated on a chair by a window,
breath a posy of heat against the
glass—into a white paper box.
The thin, wire handles are lifted

up so the box can be carried by a
man, pebbled with sleet, across a
square glass ashtray filled with
snow. He taps his hands against
his jacket pockets, his trouser
pockets. Sailor, tinker, tourist;

which is he? Here a pillow, a
suitcase. Here a road and a
fence he kneels beside to tie
his shoe lace, a tail of air
rattling up from his throat to
blossom as breath between her lips.

ACKNOWLEDGEMENTS

"The Day's Extortion," "Cowboy," *Brooding the Heartland: Poets of the Midwest*. Bottom Dog Press. "Justin's Cat," *American Poets Say Goodbye to the 20th Century*, FourWallsEightWindows. "Winter 1, 3," *Sister Stew*, Bamboo Ridge. *Violence of Potatoes*, chapbook, Ridgeway Press. Poems have also appeared in *Mānoa, Hawaii Review, Tinfish, River Styx, The Exquisite Corpse, waves, Gutenberg Review, Hanging Loose, The Alternative Press, New American Writing, Boundary 2, Caprice*.

Poems from *Who Shall Know Them?*, Viking Penguin, 1985; included by permission, Penguin Putnam: "I Don't Know Her," "The Horse," "Kitchen," "Who Is She?," "The River," "River Hill Café," "Billboards and Frame Houses," "The Crossroads," "Look at Her:," and "I Was Dragged Down." Poems from *All These Voices*, Coffee House Press, 1986; included by permission: "When Speech Comes," "A Tale of Dolors," "Still Life," "Breath," "Wife," "Woman," "The Clothesline," "What He Wanted," "Do You Know What They Did to Grandpa?," "The Bed He Dreamed Himself Into," "Inheritance," and "November." Drawings by Faye Kicknosway from the Coffee House Press 1986 calendar included by permission.

Without the help of the staff and resources of *Mānoa Journal*, there would have been no disk, no CD-ROMs, no hardcopy, and therefore no book.

Those I owe thanks and gratitude to are:

Brent Fujinaka, who scanned the drawings.

197

Amber Stierli, who scanned the manuscript.

Naomi Long, who proofread it.

Kathy Matsueda, who, with a surgeon's eye, lifted the manuscript from the gobbly-gook the scanner made of it.

Liana Holmberg, who formatted the manuscript, prepared the drawings, and calmed me. Her excitement about the book helped me believe it would have a life after machinery.

Frank Stewart who is *Mānoa*. He was calm and generous and continued to be so, especially when I was the most wild-eyed, lamenting computers should be killed from the earth. "It's all right. It's going to be fine," he'd say. "There's no problem."

Rob Wilson, look what you did. "It's alive! It's alive!" Thanks.

Poet and visual artist Faye Kicknosway was shortlisted for the Pulitzer Prize in 1985 for *Who Shall Know Them?* (Viking Penguin, 1985) and has received various other awards including the NEA Fellowship for Poetry and a P.E.N. Fiction Award. A contributor to the seminal anthology, *No More Masks!* edited by Florence Howe and Ellen Bass (Doubleday, 1973), Kicknosway has written many books, including: *O. You Can Walk on the Sky? Good.* (Capra, 1972), *Poem Tree* (Red Hanrahan Press, 1973), *A Man Is a Hook. Trouble* (Capra, 1974), *Nothing Wakes Her* (Oyster Press, 1978), *The Cat Approaches* (Alternative Press, 1978), *Asparagus, Asparagus, Ah Sweet Asparagus* (Toothpaste Press, 1981), *She Wears Him Fancy in Her Night Braid* (Toothpaste Press, 1983), *Who Shall Know Them?* (Viking Penguin, 1985), *All These Voices: Selected Poems* (Coffee House Press, 1986), *The Violence of Potatoes* (Ridgeway Press, 1990) and *Listen to Me* (Ridgeway Press, 1992). Her poems and essays have appeared in the journals *Boundary 2*, *Tri-Quarterly*, *Massachusetts Review*, *Paris Review*, *Nimrod*, *Prairie Schooner*, and in *Night Errands: How Poets Use Dreams*, edited by Roderick Townley (University of Pittsburgh Press, 1999). She earned her B.A. from Wayne State University and her M.A. from San Francisco State College. Known now to her students as Morgan Blair, she teaches at the University of Hawai'i at Manoa.

Library of Congress Cataloging-in-Publication Data
Kicknosway, Faye.
Mixed plate : new and selected poems / Faye Kicknosway.
    p.    cm.—(Wesleyan poetry)
ISBN 0–8195–6655–1 (cloth : alk. paper) — ISBN 0–8195–6656–X
(pbk. : alk. paper)
I. Title. II. Series.
PS 3561.I32M59 2003
811′.54—dc21                                              2003009966